LUFTWAFFE

Crash Archive

A DOCUMENTARY HISTORY OF EVERY
ENEMY AIRCRAFT BROUGHT DOWN
OVER THE UNITED KINGDOM

VOLUME THREE

30th **AUGUST** 1940

-

9th **SEPTEMBER** 1940

THE LUFTWAFFE CRASH ARCHIVE SERIES

Author: Nigel Parker

Editor: Simon W Parry   simon@redkitebooks.co.uk

Designer: Mark Postlethwaite   mark@redkitebooks.co.uk

Maps & Emblems: Amy Shore   www.amyshorephotography.com

Aircraft profiles: Chris Sandham-Bailey   www.inkworm.com

Specialist editors: Andy Saunders, Philippa Wheeler,
John Vasco, Milan Krajči

Contributors

Alan Brown	Clive Ellis	Steve Hall
(Deceased)	Peter Foote	Ian Hutton
Pat Burgess	(Deceased)	Gareth Jones
(Deceased)	John Foreman	John B Trim
Peter Cornwell	Chris Goss	Steve Vizard

VOLUME ONE
September 1939
-
14th August 1940

VOLUME TWO
15th August 1940
-
29th August 1940

Both available now directly from the publisher.

First Edition
ISBN 978-1-908757-08-1

First published 2013.
Red Kite
PO Box 223, Walton-on-Thames,
Surrey, KT12 3YQ
England
Tel. 0845 095 0346

Printed by
Dimograf, Sp. Z o. o. Poland

Purchase this and other Red Kite books directly from
Red Kite's websites;

www.redkitebooks.co.uk
www.wingleader.co.uk

DESIGNER'S INTRODUCTION

Welcome to Volume Three of the Luftwaffe Crash Archive. When we first started planning this series, we decided to strive to find a copy of every photo that was taken of downed Luftwaffe aircraft in the UK. Clearly this was an impossible task but we are confident that this is the biggest collection ever assembled and published to date. As such, I've tried to include every photo we have, regardless of quality, as some may contain just that small detail that a modeller or historian has been looking for. This means that for the busy periods, such as here, early September 1940, we have only been able to cover 11 days in the 128 pages of Volume Three. The extensive photographic coverage for this period is a result of several factors, the principal one of course being the amount of aircraft coming down on a daily basis. Another significant factor is that most came down in daylight thus affording the pilot an opportunity to force land his aircraft relatively intact. Move on 6 months to the height of the Blitz and most crash sites are just smoking holes as even the most experienced pilot wouldn't risk a forced landing at night in an unlit field!

For artists and modellers the biggest interest is in the colours, markings and camouflage of these aircraft. As most of the photographic coverage is in black and white, the intelligence reports that were written on the spot by trained eye-witnesses are priceless. There are of course some mistakes, mainly due to transcription errors as the reports were phoned through to the central office, but generally they should be taken as the most reliable description of how these aircraft really looked on that day.

An interesting topic of discussion amongst Luftwaffe enthusiasts has always been the use of yellow tactical markings on Bf109s during the Battle of Britain. These were introduced initially around mid-August in the form of yellow wing-tips, tailplane tips and rudder tips, presumably to aid quick identification. (The RAF reintroduced underwing roundels on its fighters at the same time for a similar reason). This soon progressed to painting the entire nose yellow, or orange as several reports describe it, making the 109s instantly recognisable from a considerable distance. Then, on 2nd September, something odd happens. All those yellow markings are replaced by white, (at least on the crashed examples examined by the Intelligence Officers). This lasts for four days until 7th September when yellow suddenly and comprehensively appears again.

There are many enthusiasts who have explained away this white marking as the Intelligence Officer's mis-interpretation of pale yellow. However, seeing the reports set out in chronological order here, it is clear that an order to overpaint the yellow with white went out to some, if not all units, at the beginning of September. In fact, it is noted on page 350 that the Bf109 of 6/LG2 had *White rudder, wing tips, the white having been painted on yellow.*

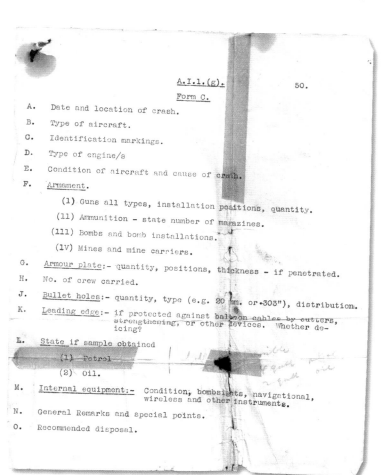

It is not in the remit of this series to investigate this any further, but we hope that in presenting the intelligence reports and photos in this chronological format, readers will be inspired to delve further into the archives to find more about this fascinating period of our history.

This research of course was started on those summer days in 1940 by the men of the RAF Air Intelligence branch. We are delighted to be able to present in this volume, pages from one of these men's diary, S John Peskett. He was tasked with visiting many of the Bf110 crash sites in Essex in early September and in all cases, he made notes based upon the form seen here to the left. Having made his notes, he would then phone this information back to the central office in London where it would be typed up as the official report. Those journeys around south-east England with the Battle still raging overhead and with most road signs removed must have been quite an adventure, especially without the modern comfort of motorways and sat-navs!

In these circumstances, the fact that John Peskett and his colleagues managed to record as much as they did, (whilst also carefully recording their expenses in the same notebook!), is a tribute to the British character when under pressure. We therefore respectfully dedicate this volume to all of them.

Left: The A.I. 1 (g) Form C, which formed the basis for all the crash investigators' reports.

LUFTWAFFE MARKING SYSTEM

The Luftwaffe code system was quite straightforward and RAF Air Intelligence quickly worked out a full list of codes and their respective units. In fact, many of the reports base the unit on the codes observed on the aircraft, usually with 100% accuracy.

During the Battle of Britain, there were two main coding systems, one for single engined fighters, the other for bombers, reconnaissance aircraft and twin engined fighters.

BOMBERS, RECCE AND HEAVY FIGHTERS

These aircraft generally used a four character code system consisting of a letter and number to the left of the fuselage cross and two letters to the right of the cross. The first two characters indicated the Geschwader, (see volume one), the third letter was the individual code for that aircraft and the fourth letter indicated the Staffel or Stab.

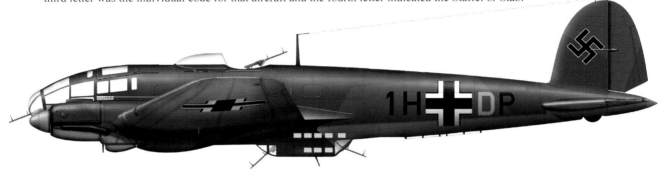

So for this Heinkel 111 the 1H is the code for KG26, the 'D' is the individual aircraft letter and the 'P' indicates the 6th Staffel. The individual aircraft letter was often painted or outlined in the staffel colour. This colour was also often applied to the aircraft's spinners as in this example. Many bomber units also carried the Kampfgeschwader emblem which would often vary in coloured background between gruppen. This aircraft has the KG26 lion emblem in red indicating II Gruppe.

There were exceptions of course, for example LG1 and LG2 using I Gruppe letters for its 13,14 and 15th Staffeln. However, the tables below serve as a guide to the majority of aircraft that took part in the Battle of Britain.

GRUPPE COLOURS - USUALLY APPLIED TO EMBLEMS OR FUSELAGE STRIPES.
Geschwader Stab - Green
I Gruppe - White
II Gruppe - Red
III Gruppe - Yellow
IV Gruppe - Blue

STAFFEL LETTERS AND COLOURS.
(4TH LETTER IN CODE - COLOUR APPLIED TO THIRD LETTER IN CODE)

LETTER	UNIT	COLOUR
A	Geschwader Stab	blue
B	I Gruppe Stab	green
C	II Gruppe Stab	green
D	III Gruppe Stab	green
F	IV Gruppe Stab	green
H	1 Staffel, I Gruppe	white
K	2 Staffel, I Gruppe	red
L	3 Staffel, I Gruppe	yellow
M	4 Staffel, II Gruppe	white
N	5 Staffel, II Gruppe	red
P	6 Staffel, II Gruppe	yellow
R	7 Staffel, III Gruppe	white
S	8 Staffel, III Gruppe	red
T	9 Staffel, III Gruppe	yellow
U	10 Staffel, IV Gruppe	white
V	11 Staffel, IV Gruppe	red
W	12 Staffel, IV Gruppe	yellow

LUFTWAFFE MARKING SYSTEM

SINGLE ENGINED FIGHTERS

In the Battle of Britain, the only aircraft type operating in this capacity was the Messerschmitt Bf109. The marking system for these fighters was simpler than for the bombers but still included the basic colour distinctions which had been used by German military units for years.

Most Bf109s were marked with a number between the cockpit and the fuselage cross, usually between 1 and 14. The colour of the number related to the Staffel colour although many examples carried black numbers;

1. Staffel,	**4. Staffel,**	**7. Staffel,**	**white number**
2. Staffel,	**5. Staffel,**	**8. Staffel,**	**red number**
3. Staffel,	6. Staffel,	9. Staffel,	yellow number

Senior Officers had symbols instead of numbers on their aircraft. There was a lot of variation between individuals but the basic symbols were as follows.

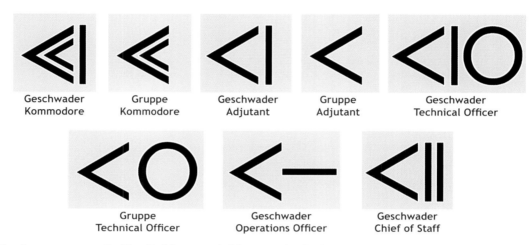

Geschwader Kommodore	Gruppe Kommodore	Geschwader Adjutant	Gruppe Adjutant	Geschwader Technical Officer

Gruppe Technical Officer	Geschwader Operations Officer	Geschwader Chief of Staff

The Gruppe was usually identified by a symbol between the fuselage cross and the tail. This, combined with the colour of the number would then accurately identify the Staffel number. In addition, most fighters carried a Geschwader emblem and/or a Staffel emblem. One notable exception was the Bf109s of LG2 which operated in a fighter-bomber capacity. They carried a black triangle symbol, usually forward of the fuselage cross, and a letter instead of a number to identify the individual aircraft.*

see page 350.

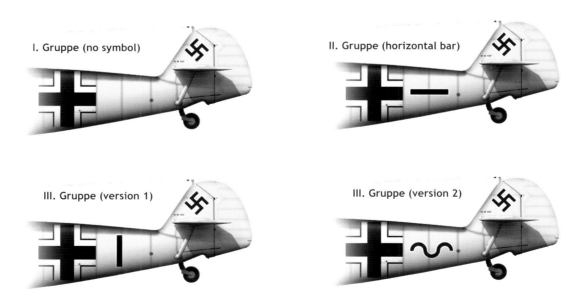

I. Gruppe (no symbol)

II. Gruppe (horizontal bar)

III. Gruppe (version 1)

III. Gruppe (version 2)

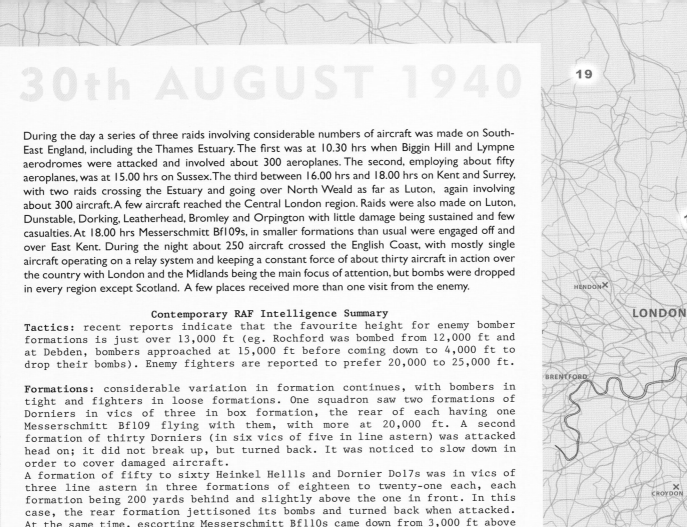

During the day a series of three raids involving considerable numbers of aircraft was made on South-East England, including the Thames Estuary. The first was at 10.30 hrs when Biggin Hill and Lympne aerodromes were attacked and involved about 300 aeroplanes. The second, employing about fifty aeroplanes, was at 15.00 hrs on Sussex. The third between 16.00 hrs and 18.00 hrs on Kent and Surrey, with two raids crossing the Estuary and going over North Weald as far as Luton, again involving about 300 aircraft. A few aircraft reached the Central London region. Raids were also made on Luton, Dunstable, Dorking, Leatherhead, Bromley and Orpington with little damage being sustained and few casualties. At 18.00 hrs Messerschmitt Bf109s, in smaller formations than usual were engaged off and over East Kent. During the night about 250 aircraft crossed the English Coast, with mostly single aircraft operating on a relay system and keeping a constant force of about thirty aircraft in action over the country with London and the Midlands being the main focus of attention, but bombs were dropped in every region except Scotland. A few places received more than one visit from the enemy.

Contemporary RAF Intelligence Summary

Tactics: recent reports indicate that the favourite height for enemy bomber formations is just over 13,000 ft (eg. Rochford was bombed from 12,000 ft and at Debden, bombers approached at 15,000 ft before coming down to 4,000 ft to drop their bombs). Enemy fighters are reported to prefer 20,000 to 25,000 ft.

Formations: considerable variation in formation continues, with bombers in tight and fighters in loose formations. One squadron saw two formations of Dorniers in vics of three in box formation, the rear of each having one Messerschmitt Bf109 flying with them, with more at 20,000 ft. A second formation of thirty Dorniers (in six vics of five in line astern) was attacked head on; it did not break up, but turned back. It was noticed to slow down in order to cover damaged aircraft.
A formation of fifty to sixty Heinkel He111s and Dornier Do17s was in vics of three line astern in three formations of eighteen to twenty-one each, each formation being 200 yards behind and slightly above the one in front. In this case, the rear formation jettisoned its bombs and turned back when attacked. At the same time, escorting Messerschmitt Bf110s came down from 3,000 ft above and started to circle round each formation, ten fighters to each lot.
Fighters generally adopted in-line formations, some circling above the bombers and others weaving from side to side. There was one case of Messerschmitt Bf109s being in front and below the bombers (which were Messerschmitt Bf110s) followed by further Messerschmitt Bf109s in the rear*.

*Almost certainly the Biggin Hill raid carried out by Erpr.Gr.210.

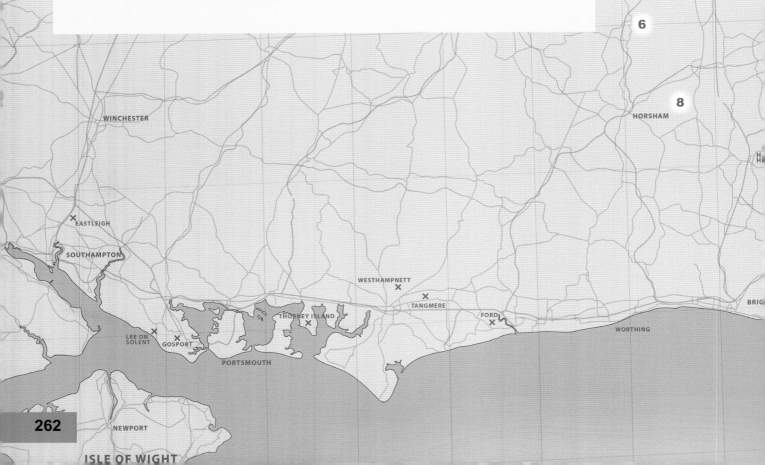

BISHOP'S
STORTFORD

15

NORTH
WEALD ✕

STAPLEFORD
TAWNEY ✕

BRENTWOOD

HORNCHURCH ✕

12

COLCHESTER

CLACTON

CHELMSFORD

17

11 ✕ ROCHFORD

SOUTHEND

SHEERNESS

14

GRAVESEND ✕

EASTCHURCH ✕

1

✕ ROCHESTER

SITTINGBOURNE

2

4

IGGIN HILL

DETLING ✕

CANTERBURY

MANSTON ✕
13

DEAL

SEVENOAKS

WEST MALLING ✕

MAIDSTONE

10

TONBRIDGE

3

ASHFORD

DOVER

TUNBRIDGE
WELLS

✕ HAWKINGE

FOLKESTONE

LYMPNE ✕

9

7

DUNGENESS

HAILSHAM

HASTINGS

BEXHILL

Miles

5   10   15

EASTBOURNE

BEACHY HEAD

| 30 August 1940 | Bf109E-4 | Wn.2765 | - +1 | 4/JG2 | MAP ID I (page 262) |

Walderslade, Chatham, Kent. 16.55 hrs.

Attacked by fighters and the pilot baled out, but his parachute failed.
Markings: nose of aircraft yellow.
ID: 57002, AW: white, Zerbst, 22/1/40, FP: -.
Ff: Ofw Karl-Heinz Harbauer +. CC 1/58.

The pilot had a notebook that showed that he had five years service and at the outbreak of war was serving with 3/JG3, before being posted to 4/JG2 on 25th November 1939. His ID disc was also for 4/JG2.

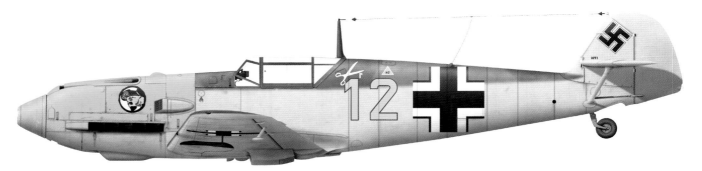

| 30 August 1940 | Bf109E-1 | Wn.3771 | 12+ | 3/JG27 | MAP ID 2 (page 262) |

Westwood Court, near Faversham, Kent. 16.45 hrs.

Started on a free-lance patrol at 16.00 hrs. Surprised in an attack by Spitfires which hit the radiator and the pilot forced landed the aircraft in good condition. About thirteen .303 strikes traced in the aircraft Markings: 12+ in yellow. Engine cowling painted orange. Shield; Tiger's Head with map of Africa as background. A plate indicated that aircraft was constructed by Fieseler, werke nr. 3271 dated 1939.
ID: 60327, AW: white, Düsseldorf, 10/1/40, FP: L 39553 Frankfurt.
Ff: Fw Ernst Arnold EKII.

The pilot had fought in Spain during the Spanish Civil War.

The interesting thing about this intelligence report is the clear differentiation between the colour of the cowling (orange), and the colour of the 12 (yellow).

The scissors + r emblem represents the name Scherer in German. This was the name of one of 3/JG27's pilots, Ulrich Scherer, who had gone missing over the Channel in July.

A selection of photos showing Fw Ernst Arnold (above) and his 'Yellow 12' which was put on display to the British public in Exeter shortly afterwards.

The yellow triangle above the 2 is the fuel cap symbol containing the octane number for the fuel, in this case, 87.

Below; Arnold's 109 carried the famous I/JG27 emblem of the lioness and native superimposed on a map of Africa.

| 30 August 1940 | Bf109E-1 | Wn.6270 | 6 + | 3/JG27 | **MAP ID 3** (page 262) |

Park House, Westwell, Ashford, Kent. 17.00 hrs.

While on a free-lance patrol, attacked by fighters and hit in the radiator, so the pilot made a good forced landing. Very few .303 strikes traced in the fuselage and wings but one through each airscrew blade and spinner.

Markings: 6 in yellow. The whole of the engine cowling back to the cockpit was painted orange and a third of the circumference of the spinner was painted yellow. Shield; Tiger's Head and map of Africa.

Camouflage: light green mottle on upper surfaces, normal blue lower surfaces.

Armament: four MG17. Standard armour plate bulkhead, but no armour to protect the pilot.

ID: 60327, AW: white, Düsseldorf, 16/1/40, FP: L 39553.

Ff: Obltn Erwin Axthelm.

Below Left: Obltn Erwin Axthelm.
Below: The I/JG27 emblem inspired by its first Gruppenkommandeur Helmut Riegel who was born in German South West Africa.

| 30 August 1940 | Bf109E-4 | Wn.1643 | White 5 + | Stab II/JG54 | **MAP ID 4** (page 262) |

Layhams Farm, Addington, Surrey. 11.25 hrs.

The pilot of this aircraft resolutely refused all information. It is believed that he collided with another aircraft during combat.

Markings: 5 in white.

ID: 71121, AW: grey, Würzburg, 13/2/40, FP: L 36849.

Ff: Ltn Rudolf Ziegler.

This pilot had in his possession a paper marked 'Battle Headquarters 29.4.40' stating that he was specifically ordered to use the belt ammunition against aircraft and balloons. The pilot stated that this was because the belts contained incendiary ammunition 'P.m.K.'. In view of the ground straffing of troops during the Dutch and French Campaigns this paper was probably issued in case the pilot was captured.

Right: Squadron Leader John Ellis of 610 Squadron stares menacingly at the camera whilst inspecting the wreckage of White 5 at Layhams Farm.

More views of the Layhams Farm crash site, this time with Squadron Leader Ellis in a more convivial mood! The pilot holding the object above is Pilot Officer Peter Lamb, with Pilot Officer Rees behind him.

Fickleshole Farm, Chelsham, Surrey. 11.55 hrs.

Started at 11.20 hrs on a free-lance patrol. Pilot was just getting into a position to attack a Hurricane, when his aircraft was rammed by some other aircraft which cut off the tail and he baled out at nearly 20,000 ft.

Markings: 6 in white. Camouflage: grey and green upper surfaces, duck egg blue underneath and yellow spinner.

Armament: two shell guns and two MG17s.

ID: 65168, AW: -, FP: L 36849.

Ff: Obltn Hans Rath EKII.

The pilot who was an Austrian had been flying with the Austrian Army but had been in Germany since the Anschluss. He had taken part in the Polish Campaign, since when he had been continually on the Western Front.

Left: The wreckage of Hans Rath's Bf109 at Fickleshole Farm. The circular object in the foreground of the lower photo is a 20mm cannon ammunition drum. The wing in the foreground is the inverted starboard wing with the leading edge slat prominent at the top.

Swires Farm, Newdigate, Surrey. 11.12 hrs.

Place of start was Nijmegen, Holland. Before reaching their objective, the crew having become separated from their formation by a previous Spitfire attack, were rammed by a Spitfire*. The Spitfire pilot was safe. Aircraft was totally destroyed.
Engines: Jumo 211.
ID: 53552, AW: white, 3/4/40, FP: L 19828 Münster.
Ff: Obltn Paul Fröhlisch.
Bo: Hptm Rudolf Bäss very badly injured. Staffelkapitän.
Bf: Ofw Waldemar Hornig +. CC 1/430.
Ofw Günther Stahlberg +. CC 1/429.
Gefr Dr Karl Heimel 53552/38 +. CC 1/428.

The Feldpostnummer was identified as IV/KG1 and the ID disc as KG1, while the Ausweis had the characteristic scratching out of the place of issue. The pilot refused to give any information but a notebook showed that he had been flying various aircraft with the V4+ - K code, although the observer claimed the aircraft was V4+BK. The pilot's Ausweis showed that on 3rd April 1940 he was an Oberfeldwebel but now an Oberleutnant.

* It is now known that this was the Hurricane flown by Flying Officer Morris of 79 Squadron.

Below: The hole made by a fully laden Heinkel 111 after it lost a wing and crashed at Swires Farm. Four bombs exploded minutes after the crash and another three were found the next day. A wing panel and the tailwheel are some of few identifiable items left for the investigators.

Roy Hill, Blackboys, near Uckfield, Sussex. 11.25 hrs.

Started from Nijmegen, Holland. Target was to bomb Farnborough aerodrome with three 250 kg and eight 50 kg bombs. Before reaching their objective they were attacked by Spitfires and the port engine shot up, so turned southwards. Attacked again by three Spitfires as well as AA fire, the crew baled out at odd intervals between Tonbridge Wells and Pevensey. One wing was torn off on crashing and remainder of the aircraft burnt.

Markings: black D outside of wing crosses.
ID: 53544 & 53545, AW: white, Erfurt, 9/5/40 & 17/7/40, FP: L 19828.
Ff: Ofw Kurt Riemann badly wounded.
Bo: Fw Richard Keter wounded.
Bf: Uffz Werner Stein.
Bm: Ofw Karl-Heinz Rauschert, Spanish Cross in Silver +. CC 1/89.
Bs: Flieger Rudolf Zinnögger 53544/69 +. CC 1/88.

One of the crew had a piece of headed notepaper dated 21st May 1940 headed 6/KG (Hindenburg) 1. The ID discs were for the 1st and 2nd Staffeln and the Feldpostnummer was for IV/KG1.

5/Kampfgeschwader I on 30th August 1940.
Although the attacks on 30th August 1940 took part in some strength with a considerable Messerschmitt Bf110 escort, only five aircraft from II/KG1 took part and all were shot down. The targets for the day were aerodromes including Farnborough and Brooklands. The diary found on one airman indicated that they had attacked Rochester on 16th August 1940, Biggin Hill on 18th & 21st August 1940 and Canterbury on 24th August 1940.

From the East Sussex Police Report it appeared that the body of the gunner was found burning in a wood, 100 yards from the wreck while that of the flight engineer was under the plane.
The personal possessions of Richard Vester were listed as follows:
One flying helmet, three gloves, one multi-lead pencil, one wrist watch (broken), one sicrostyle pencil, one bottle of rum, one Very Light cartridge, one Mauser automatic pistol number 6546, fourteen rounds of 35 ammunition, two dictionaries; German-English and German-French, one identity disc, one leather pouch containing a lucky charm and two one Pfennig pieces. One leather wallet containing identity papers, 130 Marks, a smaller wallet containing slips of paper and pencil. Another wallet containing personal papers, one diary and sundry personal papers. One small leather purse containing seven, two Franc pieces, four, one Franc pieces, four, ten Pfennig pieces and one, five Pfennig piece, one five Franc note, one two Reichmark note and one, one Reichmark note. Four handkerchiefs, two toilet combs and one tooth comb. A packet of Craven A cigarettes (gift from English folk), one petrol lighter, one wrist watch, one flying suit, one pair of flying boots, one life jacket, one brown leather satchel containing maps, one dark leather satchel, one canvas and iron bag.
One Mauser automatic pistol No. 533332 and seven rounds of ammunition were in possession of the pilot, who had been sent to Tunbridge Wells Hospital.
The dead were originally interred at Uckfield Cemetery on 4th September.

Below: The wreck of V4+DW on Roy Hill, the two dead crew members were buried initially in Uckfield cemetery.

Lower Beeding, Sussex. 11.30 hrs.

Started at 09.15 hrs from Nijmegen, Holland to attack British aerodromes. Flew direct to the target at 16,000 ft but attacked by Spitfires before reaching their objective. Hit in the port engine, and then either in an ammunition drum or petrol tank, as an explosion occurred and the plane crashed.
Shield: diamond with red and black stripes.
Armament: six 50 kg and two 250 kg bombs carried.
ID: Fliegerersatzabteilung 61, II/JG26 –Stabs Kette & 53577, AW: white, 3/4/40, FP: L 13926.
Ff: Obltn Paul Wächter 53578/60 +. CC 1/19.
Bo: Gefr Herbert Strüger wounded.
Bf: Gefr Wilhelm Hofer.
Bm: Gefr Günther Malbeck 3/FL625 +. CC 1/25.
Bs: Ogefr Walter Mönninghoff wounded.

The wireless operator was on his first War Flight and claimed that he did not like flying. He was twenty-one years old and spent twenty months in the German Air Force. His service was:
Six months Nachrichtentruppe, Vienna (mainly infantry training).
Nine months Nachrichtentruppe, Vienna as a cook.
Three weeks wireless telegraphy training in sending and receiving at the Luftnachrichtenschule, Halle.
Three weeks drafted from one aerodrome to another drilling and most of the time in railway trains.

The gunner's diary showed that in January 1940 he was posted from the Grosse Kampffliegerschule at Hörsching, near Linz to Ausbildungsgruppe 22 at Wels. At the end of March he commenced flying training at Gmunden and on the 30th April 1940 was posted to II/JG26. On 5th May 1940 he moved to an aerodrome at Märkisch, Friedland which he described as *'the end of the earth, 20 km from anywhere'*. A complaint was noted that the flying personnel were given no flying and treated as a labour corps. Three weeks later he was again moved to Quedlinburg and remained there until posted to 5/KG1 on 16th August 1940. He made his first War Flight on 24th August and his second on 27th August from which they returned with seven bullet holes in the aircraft, another two aircraft having to make forced landings. On his third War Flight he was shot down.

Special Constable SC804 Stephen Knight reported:
At 11.30 hrs on 30/8/40 I was on duty at at Stonewick, Warninglid, when I saw a German bomber falling to the west. I kept observation and saw two men come down by parachute. One of these landed at Eastlands, Warninglid. I went up to him and he put up his right arm and said 'Kamerad'. Upon searching him I found he had a broken left forearm. One other airman landed further south and was detained by a cowman with a pitchfork.
The two dead airmen were originally buried at Hill's cemetery, Horsham.

Right: A man poses with what appears to be a section of fuselage skin from the He111 at Lower Beeding.

| 30 August 1940 | He111H-2 | Wn.5125 | V4+HV | 5/KG1 | MAP ID 9 (page 262) |

At sea - six miles off Folkestone, Kent. 14.22 hrs.

Flying with a large force of bombers and Messerschmitt Bf110s, about ten miles south of London, en-route to Farnborough aerodrome, they were attacked by a Spitfire. With one engine shot up pilot turned back, but they were attacked again over the coast when alone by three Spitfires and the other engine stopped. The pilot put the aircraft down on the water near a motor boat and crew was brought into Dover.
ID: 53552, AW: white on grey cloth, 3/4/40, FP: L 19828.
Ff: Uffz Emil Burger EKII.
Bo: Gefr Heinz Hildebrandt.
Bf: Gefr Walter Feierbend wounded.
Bm: Gefr Herbert Roggemann.
Bs: Gefr Willi Klappholz wounded.

The unit was assumed from the Feldpostnummer to be IV/KG1, while the ID disc was associated with 10/KG1, along with the Ausweis that had the characteristic scratching out of the place of issue. Until the end of June 1940 the flight engineer had been with 1/KG1 and had the Feldpostnummer L 02110 of I/KG1.

| 30 August 1940 | He111H-2 | Wn.3305 | V4+MV | 5/KG1 | MAP ID 10 (page 262) |

Haxted, near Lingfield, Surrey. 11.35 hrs.

About twenty aircraft started at 10.15 hrs from Nijmegen, Holland with an objective stated to be hangars on Farnborough aerodrome. The objective was bombed from 13,000 ft but they were immediately attacked by Spitfires, which damaged both engines and started a small fire. The pilot made a good forced landing.
Shield: white diamond in circle with solid red diamond in centre. Aircraft was delivered 1st April 1940.
Engines: Jumo 211. .303 strikes found in the oil radiators.
Armament: twenty 50 kg bombs carried.
ID: 53522, AW: white, Nordhausen, 3/4/40, FP: L 19828.
Ff: Fw Heinz Schnabel.
Bo: Gefr Hans Groth.
Bf: Uffz Erich Paeslack wounded.
Bm: Uffz Erich Stärk.
Bs: Gefr Walter Reis 53552/44 +. CC 1/434.
Air Intelligence recorded the aircraft code as V4+MV, this would normally represent 11. Staffel but according to Luftwaffe records this and the other V coded Heinkels lost on this day were with 5. Staffel.

Above: The red diamond emblem carried by the Haxted Heinkel. Below: The oil spattered starboard engine gives a clue to the demise of the otherwise immaculate V4+MV down at Haxted.

Lifstan Way, Southend-on-Sea, Essex. 16.35 hrs.

Started from St. Omer at 15.15 hrs to attack Hatfield aerodrome, north-west of London. When flying at 13,000 ft in Ketten Vic before reaching their objective they were attacked from all sides by Spitfires and Hurricanes. The rear gunner was wounded, then the starboard engine hit. Some of the bombs were scuttled and gradually coming down a further attack wounded two more crew. The aircraft finally caught fire, crashed on landing and burnt out.

Below: Uffz Helmut Gall.
Below right: Ltn Wolff Rösler.

Markings: J in yellow on underside of one wing. Spinners traces of red and yellow paint. Airframe no. 5532, dated May 1939.

Engines: Jumo 211-B one numbered 50460.
Armament: four MG15 recovered. Two 250 kg and six 50 kg bombs still on board. Both high explosive and incendiary bombs carried. No armour found.
ID: 69039 & 69040, AW: grey, 30/5/40, FP: L 02574 Nürnberg.
Ff: Uffz Helmut Gall.
Bo: Ltn Wolff Rösler.
Bf: Fw Ernst Erhard von Kunheim +. CC 1/107.
Bm: Uffz Adolf Saam +. CC 1/108.
Bs: Uffz Otto Fischer 69040/46 +. CC 1/106.

Below: The scattered remains of A1+JL lie strewn across Lifstan Way. The photo below left shows the railway bridge that still crosses the road at this point today. Southend beach is half a mile beyond to the south.
Note the engineers already up the pole trying to reconnect the damaged wires. The trees and lamp posts have had the bases painted white to aid visibility in the blackout.

Colne Engaine, near Halstead, Essex. 16.30 hrs.

The whole of II/KG53 started from Lille to attack an aerodrome; escort provided by Messerschmitt Bf110s. They had already dropped their bombs, when this aircraft was separated from the formation and a Spitfire attacked from the front wounding the pilot. Further attacks by other Spitfires wounded or killed most of the other members of the crew and an explosion occurred, so the survivors decided to make a forced landing. Numerous .303 strikes were traced all over fuselage and wings, estimated to be about 150.

Markings: B in black with white edging; spinners red.

Engines: Jumo 211 A, starboard No. 45462 and port No. 51393.

Armament: seven MG15; two in nose, one upper rear, two lateral, two lower rear.

ID: 56116, AW: grey, Ingolstadt, 5/2/40 & grey, Einheit L 32925, 15/2/40 & 2/6/40, FP: -.

Ff: Fw Fritz Steinberg wounded.

Bo: Ofw Thomas Dietrich 65116/17 +. CC 5/325.

Bf: Fw Alois Hummel wounded.

Bm: Fw Andreas Fellner wounded.

Bs: Uffz Theo Hugelschutz .

The aircraft was stated to be only fourteen days old, having been collected new from Germany.

Left: Despite being wounded, the pilot Fritz Steinberg managed to perform a very good forced landing in A1+BN at Colne Engaine.

Goodmans Farm, near Manston aerodrome, Kent. 16.35 hrs.

Started about 14.00 hrs from an aerodrome near Armentieres to bomb an aerodrome north of London. On preliminary interrogation, it was stated that the whole of Gruppe II was at the aerodrome near Armentieres and that twelve aircraft, with an escort of Messerschmitt Bf109s took part in this raid. Intercepted at about 13,000 ft by fighters, near the River Crouch, the pilot was badly wounded and the observer took control and landed the aircraft. Possible damage also caused by AA fire. Bomb load jettisoned over the Thames.

Markings: J in yellow, 2782 in black painted on the tail.

Engines: Jumo 211 J.

Armament: seven MG15; one top aft, two lateral, two bottom gun pits (one forward, one aft), one in normal nose position and above this gun was an additional MG15 firing forward and upwards through a slot in the perspex, which could be elevated to approximately ten degrees aft of the vertical. Sixteen 50 kg bombs carried.

ID: 65117, AW: grey, Ingolstadt, 15/2/40 & white, Einheit L 32925, FP: L 06460.

Ff: Fw Karl Eckert 53576/204. Margate, Kent. Died of wounds 2nd September 1940.

Bo: Gefr Albert Klapp wounded.

Bf: Gefr Hans Köhler +. Ramsgate, Kent. Died of wounds 2nd September 1940.

Bm: Fw Kurt Stöckl.

Bs: Gefr Friedrich Gluck wounded.

The Geschwader Kommodore was said to have been shot down recently over England, although Air Intelligence had no record of this. The Staffelkapitän of 6/KG53 was Hauptmann Mund.

Right: A long unidentified photo of a Heinkel on display to the public. The distinctive 'J' and the two small bullet strikes ahead of the swastika confirm its identity as A1+JP that came down at Goodmans Farm on 30 August 1940.

Below: A1+JP neatly harvested the crop in the field at Goodmans Farm as it careered to a halt in the hands of the observer. The werke number 2782 can be seen stencilled on the rudder.

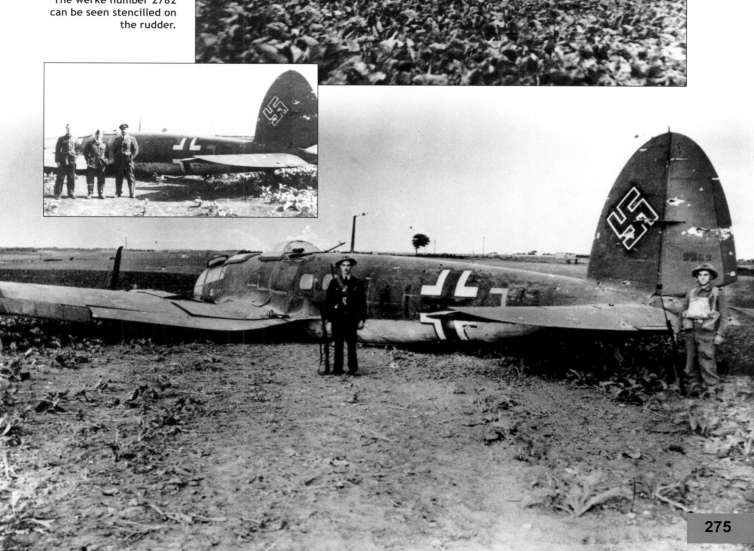

| 30 August 1940 | He111H-2 | Wn.6818 | A1+GP | 6/KG53 | **MAP ID 14** (page 262) |

At sea - off Isle of Sheppey, Kent. 16.30 hrs.

Started from Vendeville (Lille) at 15.10 hrs to bomb Radlett aerodrome, Hertfordshire. A total of eighteen aircraft took part in this flight, escorted by Messerschmitt Bf110s but before reaching their objective they were engaged in a quarter attack from the front by two fighters. The starboard engine stopped at once and the other heated up. Losing height, the bombs were scuttled and aircraft finally landed in the sea, the crew taking to their dinghy. The whole formation was turned back before reaching their objective.
Markings: G in yellow.
Armament: two 250 kg and twelve 50 kg bombs carried.
ID: 65117, AW: white, Schwäbisch Hall, 7/5/40 & 12/5/40; grey, Ingolstadt, 15/2/40 & white, L 32925, 16/6/40, FP: L 06460.
Ff: Uffz Gerhard Rascher.
Bo: Uffz Werner Roempert.
Bf: Uffz Hans Wagner.
Bm: Uffz Arthur Schall.
Bs: Uffz Gustav Keuerleben.

| 30 August 1940 | He111H-2 | Wn.2624 | A1+CR | 7/KG53 | **MAP ID 15** (page 262) |

Near 'The Rectory', Hunsdon, Hertfordshire. 16.30 hrs.

Took off from Lille at 15.00 hrs with about fifteen other aircraft to bomb Radlett aerodrome. They flew across at about 13,000 ft in Staffel Vic-astern and were intercepted about ten minutes before reaching the target. Six to seven Hurricanes attacked the formation from all sides, the starboard engine stopped, the rudder was damaged and then coming into land the port engine caught fire.
Markings: the aircraft had seventeen stripes on the rudder, said to denote the number of times this aircraft had made it to Great Britain along with the werke number 2624. C in white, C also appeared on both upper surfaces of the wing tips. Shield; a red M with a bomb through it outlined in white. Aircraft constructed by Arado, F.W. Licence Heinkel werke nr. 16/125 L. dated November 1938.
Engines: Jumo 211, one engine numbered 4519.
Armament: thirteen 50 kg bombs. The bomb load was said to be so small due to carrying an extra fuel load.
ID: 69042, AW: grey, Giebelstadt, 1/2/40, FP: L 03171 Frankfurt.
Ff: Ltn Ernst Fischbach.
Obs: Fw Wilhelm Kusserow wounded.
Bf: Fw Georg Distler wounded.
Bs: Gefr Fritz Riess 60553/84. CC 5/243. Died in the County Hospital.
Bs: Gefr Leo Stilp 69042/54. CC 5/244. Died of his wounds.

The pilot had only made six War Flights; four were reconnaissance flights over the sea and the fifth was an abortive attempt to reach North Weald aerodrome. He had previously been an Officer on a Zeppelin.

Through subsequent interrogation it was claimed that Stab II/KG53 and the 4th Staffel each lost three Heinkel He111, as a result of which the Gruppenstab was virtually wiped out and aircraft from the 4th and 5th Staffeln, with their own crews were used as Stab aircraft.

| 30 August 1940 | Bf110D-0 | Wn.3315 | A2+HK | 5/ZG2 | **MAP ID 16** (page 262) |

Rochford's Nursery, Durants Road, Ponders End, Essex. 16.50 hrs.

Shot down by Hurricanes and exploded on landing, wreckage being strewn over a wide area.
Papers found near the crash site indicated that on the 23rd and 24th July 1940 the Staffel was moving between Guyancourt and Caen and from 15th to 28th August 1940 was operating from St. Aubin.
ID: -, AW: green, Fliegerhorstkommandantur 9/VII, 16/5/40, FP: -.
Ff: Hptm Adolf Schuldt +. CC 8/100. Staffelkapitän.
Bf: Uffz Karl Dyroff +. CC 8/104.

The aircraft code was assumed from a log book found in the wreckage. The Ausweis format had not been previously encountered.

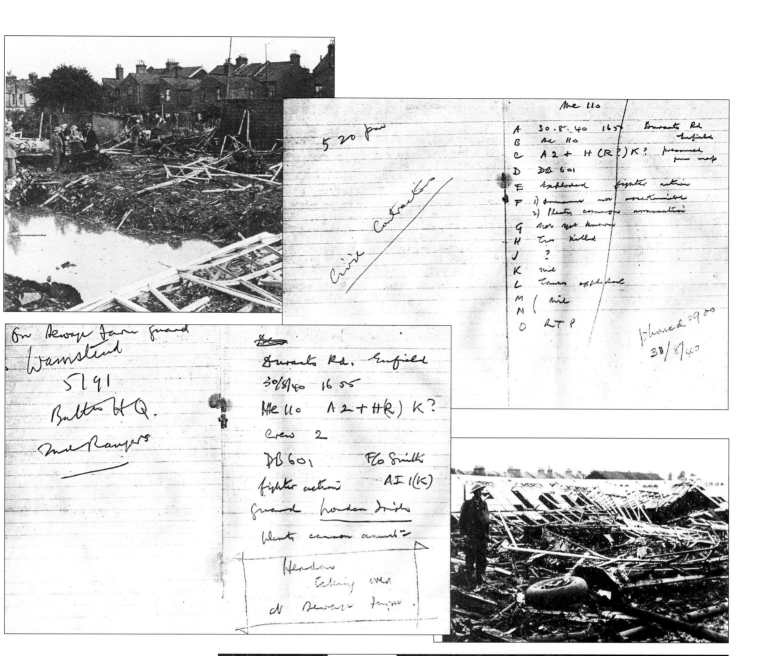

When the Air Ministry inspector John Peskett arrived at Rochford's Nursery, he was met with very little to record in his notebook! Following the template seen on page 259 his notes can be seen here.

| 30 August 1940 | Bf110C-2 | Wn.3496 | 3U+KP | 5/ZG26 | MAP ID 17 (page 262) |

Mill Hill Farm, Rettenden, Essex. 16.30 hrs.

Started at 15.00 hrs from St. Omer, escorting Heinkel He111s; the 4th, 5th and 6th Staffeln all operating together, with seventy Messerschmitt Bf110s taking part in the operation, flying in Vic-fours. The bombers did not reach their objective but were turned back and this aircraft was attacked from behind by a Hurricane. The starboard engine stopped, then the port and the pilot brought the aircraft down to make a good landing.

Markings: K in yellow on wing tips. Shield; a red diamond, with a smaller diamond inside, white edged in red.

Engines: DB 601.

ID: 60038, AW: grey, 6/3/40, FP: L 33708 Brussels.

Ff: Uffz Rudolf Franke.

Bf: Uffz Willi Hübner.

Although the aircraft was coded for the 6th Staffel, the crew was with the 5th Staffel of ZG26. *

*Franke & Hübner of 5. Staffel were not slated to fly this mission as their machine was unserviceable. However 6. Staffel had a spare machine, so they were sent to that Staffel to fly 3U+KP. Franke soon realised why 3U+KP was not used by 6. Staffel, as the engines suffered from poor performance. (source: interview by Peter Cornwell & John Vasco with Rudolf Franke)

Above: The red diamond emblem found on 3U+KP.

Below and opposite page: The wreckage of M8+BM at Enfield Sewage Farm

| 30 August 1940 | Bf110C-4 | Wn.3257 | M8+BM | 4/ZG76 | MAP ID 18 (page 262) |

Enfield Sewage Farm, Wharf Road, Ponders End, Essex. 16.55 hrs.

Aircraft shot down by a Hurricane and crashed in flames. The wireless operator was burned and the pilot killed by sixteen MG bullets.

Armament: four MG17, two 20 mm cannon, one MG15.

ID: -, AW: red, Köln, 11/3/40, signed Schiller, FP: -.

Ff: Hptm Heinz Wagner +. CC 8/101. Staffelkapitän.

Bf: Stabsfw Adolf Schmidt* 53547/8 +. CC 8/102.

The pilot was identified by his Ausweis. The aircraft markings were those of ZG76 and piece of paper refered to the 5th Staffel, II Gruppe.

* German war-time records state Heinrich Schmidt.

Right: John Peskett's notes for M8+BM. Note the question mark after the M, caused by the letter being burnt off the fuselage, as seen in the middle photo opposite. The letter B was presumably deduced from the letter on the wing.

Barley Beans Farm, Kimpton, Hertfordshire. 16.30 hrs.

Shot down in combat with fighters and the wireless operator baled out. The aircraft hit a tree and then dived into the ground at high speed and buried.

Markings: third M in white.

ID: -, AW: red, Köln, 16/7/40 & white paper on grey cloth, Nellingen, 10/1/40, FP: L 30644.

Ff: Ofw Georg Anthony +. Hitchin, Herts.

Bf: Uffz Heinrich Nordmeier, seriously injured.

The wireless operator had a dental appointment at the Advanced Treatment Centre, Le Mans on 21st August 1940.

Below and left: M8+MM exploded on impact leaving few recognisable fragments. This aircraft was shot down by Ludwik Paszkiewicz of 303 (Polish) Squadron who broke off against orders from a training mission to intercept the 110 over Luton. This first victory for the squadron led to it being declared operational the following day.

Gothaer Waggonfabrik A. G. GOTHA
Abt.: Flugzeugbau

Baumuster:	B F 110
Teil-Werk-Nr.:	110.06.5
Teil/Zeich.-Nr.:	8-110.502-02
Baujahr 193	/ Prüfz.

EXAMPLE OF A COMBAT REPORT FOUND ON THE PILOT OF A
MESSERSCHMITT BF110 OF II/ZG76

II/ZG76   **30/8/40**

Report on bringing down an enemy a/c.

1) Time (day, hour, minute) and Place: *30/8/40. 1705 hrs.   Dover.*
   Height at which shot down: *4.500 m.*

2) a/c type shot down: *Spitfire.*

3) Nationality of the enemy: *English.*
   Works No. Or Registration marks of the a/c: -.

4) Manner in which destroyed:
   a) Burning (white trail of smoke from petrol, trail of dark smoke, bright flame).
                                                       White trail of smoke from petrol.
   b) Disintergration (individual parts, explosion).
   c) Forced landing (on which side of the front, safely or with damage).
   d) Shot into flames, after being forced down on the enemy side.

5) Type of crash:
   a) On which side of the line.
   b) Vertically or at a flat angle, in flames after crashing, in a cloud of dust.
   c) Not observed, why not? *Not observed because I was being attacked by other enemy fighters.*

6) Fate of the crew (dead, baled out, not observed).

7) Account of the flight: *Detailed to escort a bomber formation of He111. Near Dover, English fighters tried to attack the bomber formation. Our Gruppe immediately formed a defensive ring above the bombers. The English fighters then tried to attack us. A Spitfire suddenly came at our machine from behind on the left and fired at us. It then made off to the right, exposing its entire side. I shot at the Spitfire and observed that it listed downwards, with a cloud of white smoke pouring from it. I was unable to pursue this a/c further, as other English fighters were attacking and I had to keep an eye on them.*

8) Witnesses:
   a) in the air.
   b) on the ground.
9) Number of attacks made on the enemy a/c.
10) Direction from which the individual attacks were made.
11) Distance from which the shooting down was started: *100 - 150 m.*
12) Tactical position from which the shooting down was undertaken.
13) Was any of the enemy gunners put out of action?
14) Kind of ammunition used: *S m k L (tracer) B Munition, S m K and P m K.*
15) Quantity of ammunition used.
16) Kind and No. of weapons used in shooting down the a/c.   *One M.G.15.*
17) Type of our own machine: *Me.110.*
18) Anything else of a tactical or technical nature worth noting.
19) Hits on own a/c: *None.*

Sig. Mutan. Uffz.

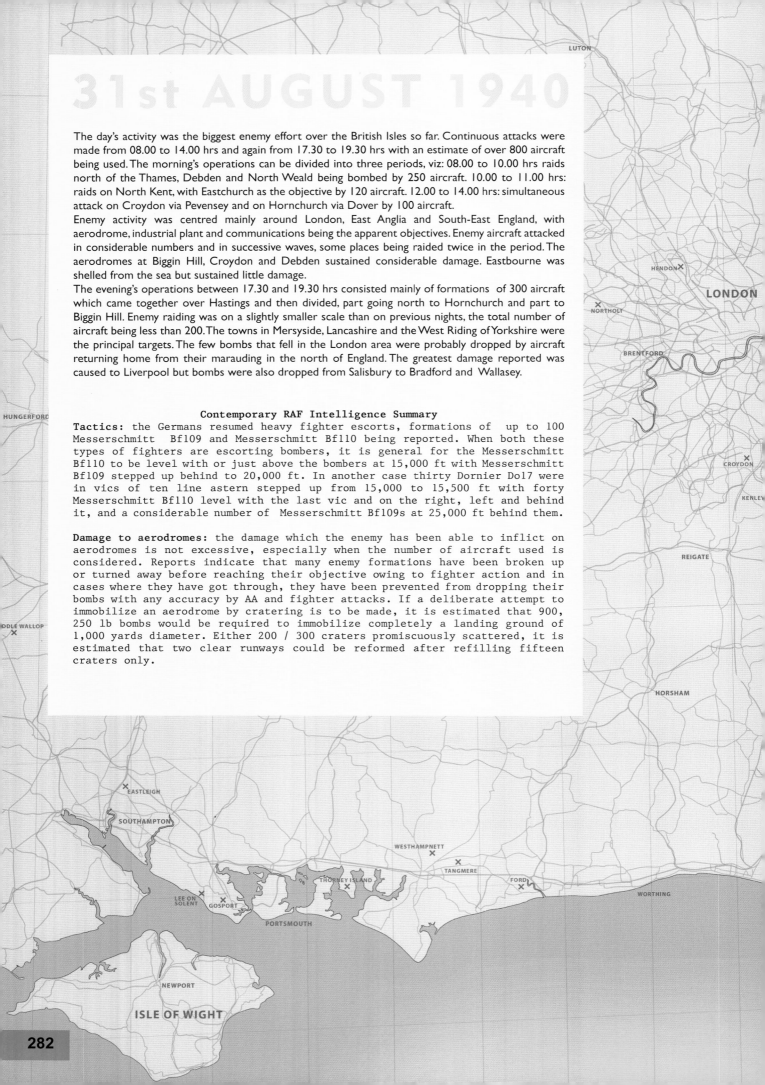

The day's activity was the biggest enemy effort over the British Isles so far. Continuous attacks were made from 08.00 to 14.00 hrs and again from 17.30 to 19.30 hrs with an estimate of over 800 aircraft being used. The morning's operations can be divided into three periods, viz: 08.00 to 10.00 hrs raids north of the Thames, Debden and North Weald being bombed by 250 aircraft. 10.00 to 11.00 hrs: raids on North Kent, with Eastchurch as the objective by 120 aircraft. 12.00 to 14.00 hrs: simultaneous attack on Croydon via Pevensey and on Hornchurch via Dover by 100 aircraft.

Enemy activity was centred mainly around London, East Anglia and South-East England, with aerodrome, industrial plant and communications being the apparent objectives. Enemy aircraft attacked in considerable numbers and in successive waves, some places being raided twice in the period. The aerodromes at Biggin Hill, Croydon and Debden sustained considerable damage. Eastbourne was shelled from the sea but sustained little damage.

The evening's operations between 17.30 and 19.30 hrs consisted mainly of formations of 300 aircraft which came together over Hastings and then divided, part going north to Hornchurch and part to Biggin Hill. Enemy raiding was on a slightly smaller scale than on previous nights, the total number of aircraft being less than 200. The towns in Merseyside, Lancashire and the West Riding of Yorkshire were the principal targets. The few bombs that fell in the London area were probably dropped by aircraft returning home from their marauding in the north of England. The greatest damage reported was caused to Liverpool but bombs were also dropped from Salisbury to Bradford and Wallasey.

Contemporary RAF Intelligence Summary

Tactics: the Germans resumed heavy fighter escorts, formations of up to 100 Messerschmitt Bf109 and Messerschmitt Bf110 being reported. When both these types of fighters are escorting bombers, it is general for the Messerschmitt Bf110 to be level with or just above the bombers at 15,000 ft with Messerschmitt Bf109 stepped up behind to 20,000 ft. In another case thirty Dornier Do17 were in vics of ten line astern stepped up from 15,000 to 15,500 ft with forty Messerschmitt Bf110 level with the last vic and on the right, left and behind it, and a considerable number of Messerschmitt Bf109s at 25,000 ft behind them.

Damage to aerodromes: the damage which the enemy has been able to inflict on aerodromes is not excessive, especially when the number of aircraft used is considered. Reports indicate that many enemy formations have been broken up or turned away before reaching their objective owing to fighter action and in cases where they have got through, they have been prevented from dropping their bombs with any accuracy by AA and fighter attacks. If a deliberate attempt to immobilize an aerodrome by cratering is to be made, it is estimated that 900, 250 lb bombs would be required to immobilize completely a landing ground of 1,000 yards diameter. Either 200 / 300 craters promiscuously scattered, it is estimated that two clear runways could be reformed after refilling fifteen craters only.

| 31 August 1940 | Bf110D-0 | Wn.3381 | S9+GK | 2/EproGr210 | **MAP ID 1** (page 282) |

Stansted, near Wrotham Hill, Kent. 13.15 hrs.

Shot down by fighters while attacking Croydon aerodrome, having just released the bombs over their target the port engine and the tail were hit. The pilot made a very good, rapid belly landing as he knew his wireless operator was wounded and hoped to save his life.

Aircraft in fair condition. Standard equipment except for bomb release at the bottom of the pilot's panel. Markings: G in black with white edging. Spinners white*. Camouflage: standard green and light blue. The usual red map of England, obscured by a bomb sight graticule was conspicuous by its absence but the pilot claimed that it was because they had not got round to painting it on all the aircraft.

Engines: DB 601.

Armament: five machine guns and two cannon found. No armour plate found.

ID: 6N.Kp. Quakenbrück, AW: -, FP: L 32337.

Ff: Uffz Ernst Glaeske.

Bf: Ogefr Konrad Schweda 99 LN.K.P.QUAKE +. CC 1/356.

The pilot had obtained his N.S.F.K. Gliding Certificate B on 27th September 1938 and joined the German Air Force soon after. At the outbreak of war he was acting as an instructor at Alt-Lönnewitz, before being transferred to the Zerstörer School at Schloissheim. He had applied for an active service posting but did not get to an operational unit until he was transferred to EproGr 210 in August 1940. His first War Flight was the attack on Manston aerodrome on 14th August 1940 and the following day was attacking Croydon aerodrome and claimed to have dropped two 250 kg bombs in the middle of a large hangar.

On 22nd August 1940 over the English Channel near Calais, France, this pilot saw what he took to be a Messerschmitt Bf109 and waved to it but to his dismay it turned out to be a Spitfire. His starboard engine was shot up and he had to struggle home on the port engine only.

*Possibly a factory applied marking that had not been overpainted with Staffel colours.

| 31 August 1940 | Bf109E-4 | Wn.5339 | | 3/JG3 | **MAP ID 2** (page 282) |

Whalebone Lane Gunsite, Chadwell Heath, Essex. 19.15 hrs.

While on a free-lance fighter operation the aircraft was shot down by fighters at high altitude and pilot baled out. Aircraft dived into the ground and burnt out.

Identification markings indecipherable but trace of letter after the cross coloured yellow, outlined in black.

Engine: DB601, No. 311002A/205-4.

ID: 55570, AW: white on blue/black, Köln, 22/5/40, FP: -.

Ff: Obltn Johann Loidolt wounded by the L.D.V.

The pilot refused to give any information claiming loss of memory, but another airman from his unit had enquired after his well-being.

| 31 August 1940 | Bf109E-4 | Wn.1082 | 4 + | 3/JG3 | **MAP ID 3** (page 282) |

Shoeburyness Beach, Essex. 18.45 hrs.

Started from France at 16.30 hrs on a free-lance patrol, at great height, two formations of eight aircraft taking part. When flying at nearly 30,000 ft this aircraft was attacked from the rear by a British aircraft. This pilot tried to climb out of danger, which the pilot thought possible but he saw his right support shot down and in diving down to see his fate, was himself hit in the engine. The aircraft was found to be in good condition.

Markings: 4 in yellow with black edges. Shield; a dragon's head with yellow snake-like body, outlined in black with a very protruding long red tongue. Three stripes on the tail represent one Morane on 13th May 1940 and two Curtiss on 14th May 1940. Aircraft constructed by Erla, Leipzig, werke nr. 1082 dated 15th July 1940.

Armament: four MGs; one MG in each wing, two firing through the airscrew from the top of the engine.

Engine: DB 601A, constructed by Daimler-Benz at Genshagen, werke nr. 60533.

ID: 55567, AW: white, Köln Ostheim, 7/3/40, FP: L 31489.

Ff: Obltn Helmut Rau. Staffelkapitän.

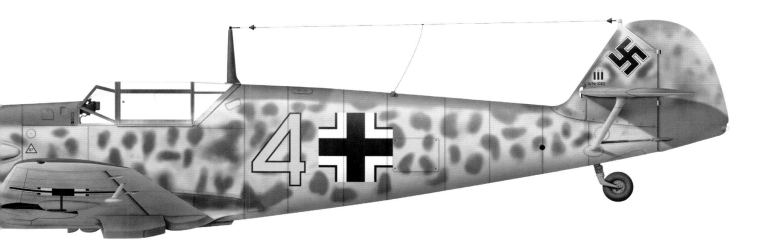

Below: Obltn Helmut Rau, the pilot of 'Yellow 4' which he force landed onto Shoeburyness beach on 31st August 1940. The aircraft was recovered relatively intact and put on display to the public, (below right).

Between Ann Street, Robert Street, Plumstead, Kent. 18.30 hrs.

While on a free-lance sortie over London this aircraft crashed possibly due to a collision in mid air and was completely burnt out.

Markings: no identification was visible beyond propeller and spinner being coloured yellow and a plate showing aircraft constructed by Erla, M.W. at Leipzig dated 31st February 1940 and a shield showing a yellow snake with red tongue.

Armament: two 20 mm cannon and two MG17 found amongst wreckage. Standard 8 mm armoured bulkhead but no armour plate for pilot's seat or head protection.

ID: 55567, AW: white, Köln, 7/3/40, FP: -.

Ff: Obltn Walter Binder 55567/6 +. CC 1/466.

Baled out, but his parachute failed and his body was found at Gibson Farm.

The unit was established from the ID disc and confirmed by a prisoner from the same unit.

Civilians gather round the buried Messerschmitt in their back gardens in Plumstead. The eye witness describes a yellow dragon with red claws being just visible. This can be seen just above one the the nearest boys' head, the aircraft is lying inverted facing the camera.

Letter written by Iris Hanaford of Plumstead.

We had some excitement the Saturday before last. A Messerschmitt 109 was brought down in Ann Street. A Spitfire was after it and a dog fight went on overhead, then down it came making a horrible row. One wing came off and sailed just over our house. Dad thought it would land in the road but it just cleared the houses on the other side of the road and landed in a garden in Hector Street. The rest of the plane crashed in the gardens of two houses. It caught fire so that it was not much to look at. The cockpit buried itself about 3ft in the ground so we were told by a fireman when we went to see it. We could only see the ends of the propeller as it was buried. There was a yellow dragon with red claws painted on the little bit of the cockpit that we could see. The rest of the plane was such a mess you couldn't tell what was what. The people started a Spitfire Fund and let people in to see it , they collected about £96. There was a fund started to see the wing too, but that was only left there for a day, so they didn't get so much.

Below: Another view of the wreckage taken from 90 degrees to the left of the previous photo.

Right: The dragon or 'Tatzelwurm' emblem was based upon an Alpine mythical creature.

Below right: John Peskett was having a very busy weekend in Essex as his notebook testifies!

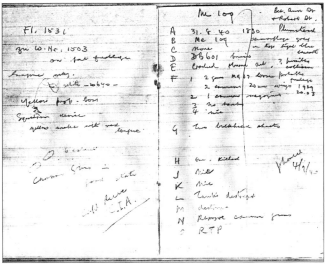

31 August 1940	Bf109E-1	Wn.3175	4/JG3	**MAP ID 5** (page 282)

At sea - off Dover, Kent.

This aircraft failed to return from a free-lance operation over the London area and was presumed to have been shot down in combat with fighters.
Ff: Ltn Richard von Larisch +. NKG. Body recovered from the sea on 13th September1940.

A prisoner of war from I/JG3 had enquired after this Officer and a document found on the body was stamped '4th Staffel'.

31 August 1940	Bf109E-4	Wn.1475	6/JG3	**MAP ID 6** (page 282)

Lydd Ranges, Dungeness, Kent. 18.30 hrs.

The formation had completed a circle, starting from Dover, passing round the south of London almost back to their starting point, many aircraft having been attacked by isolated Spitfires on the way, this pilot claiming to have shot one of them down. During the dog-fight he thought he was hit by fire from another Messerschmitt Bf109 above him and had to make a forced landing and set fire to his aircraft
ID: 57012, AW: grey, Handorf bei Münster, 13/1/40, FP: L 31407.
Ff: Obltn Karl Westerhoff EKII wounded.

The pilot gave his unit as JG3 during interrogation but neither the ID disc nor Feldpostnummer agreed. The pilot had served in the Polish and French Camapigns.

31 August 1940	Bf109E-1	Wn.708	Stab I/JG26	**MAP ID 7** (page 282)

Pitsea, Essex. 18.00 hrs.

While escorting bombers to London at 16,000 ft hit by AA fire, one wing breaking off in mid air and aircraft crashed on its back on fire.
Camouflage: slate grey upper and pale blue lower. Aircraft constructed by Arado Flugzeugwerke B.F.109, werke nr. 708 dated 1940.
Engine: DB 601 engine, crank case no. 65054.
The body of the pilot was found with an unopened parachute at Bridge Road, Rainham, Essex on 2nd September 1940.
ID: -, AW: white, Dortmund & white, Köln, 19/8/40. (The pilot had two Ausweis), FP: L 14856.
Ff: Obltn Ludwig Hafer +. CC 1/368.
The first Ausweis was linked to JG26, while the pilot's pay-book showed that he was at Jagdfliegerschule, Schleissheim on 1st September 1939 and with JG26 on 29th March 1940. The present Ausweis and Feldpostnummer were unidentified. The parachute Ausweis had date of manufacture as 27th January 1940 and was stamped 2/KG Z.b.V.172.
Some sources give this aircraft as Wn. 4806.

31 August 1940	Bf109E-1	Wn.6309	7/JG26	**MAP ID 8** (page 282)

Knatts Valley, West Kingsdown, Kent. 17.40 hrs.

Shot down by fighters during a bomber escort sortie and the aircraft broke up in the air, the pilot baled out.
Camouflage: green and grey upper surfaces, with blue under surfaces, fin and rudder.
ID: -, AW: -, FP: 39520 Brussels.
Ff: Uffz Horst Liebeck injured.

An order to collect Messerschmitt Bf109 werke nr. 6309 and stamped Sta III/JG26 was found on the pilot.

31 August 1940	Bf109E-1	Wn.3464	7/JG26	**MAP ID 9** (page 282)

Mill House Farm, Allington, Kent. 18.30 hrs.

This pilot started from Calais on escort duties in a formation with other fighters which was broken up before reaching their objective and this aircraft was reported to have been shot down by fighters, the aircraft being completely smashed.
Markings: camouflaged in grey-green top, pale blue underneath. Airframe nr. 109-3464.
ID: 60321, AW: white, Merseburg, 17/8/40, FP: 32053.
Ff: Uffz Martin Klar very badly wounded.

The ID disc was for S III/JG26. Amongst the pilot's effects were a sketch of a shield, showing a dancing bear, with a red umbrella being broken across its nose.

Jubilee Hall Farm, Ulcombe, Kent. 18.45 hrs.

While on escort duties the aircraft was attacked and shot down by Spitfires, making a good wheels-up landing.

Markings: 10 and I in yellow. Shield; a Hellhound and black gothic S on a white shield. Fuselage built by Erla werke nr. 62914. Camouflage: green upper surfaces, light blue underneath.

Armament: two MG17 under engine cowling and two 20 mm shell guns in wings.

ID: 63021, AW: grey, Dortmund, 15/1/40, FP: -.

Ff: Ltn Wilhelm Fronhöfer EKII.

The unit was assumed from the ID disc and Ausweis.

Below: Ltn Wilhelm Fronhöfer who force landed at Jubilee Farm.

The S in the shield was the famous 'Schlageter' emblem of JG26 and the 'Hellhund' was the symbol of the 9th Staffel.

Below right: Fronhöfer's 109 on display to the public.

Wagstaff Farm, two miles north-west of High Halden, Kent. 13.00 hrs.

Started at 12.20 hrs on an escort mission. A large number of fighters and bombers were flying together at about 16,000 ft somewhere just outside London when a big dog-fight developed and this aircraft was attacked by two Spitfires and one Hurricane. The engine was hit and damaged, so the pilot dived right down and a long chase developed over Maidstone, finally the engine stopped and the pilot made a forced landing in a field, the aircraft being in good condition. The bombers had not reached their objective when they were attacked.

Markings: 13 in white. The nose of this aircraft was painted yellow. Armament two MG17 and two 20 mm cannon.

ID: 58201, AW: white on grey cloth, Köln Ostheim, 8/1/40, FP: L 37066. Ff: Obltn Hans-Jurgen Ehrig EKI. Staffelkapitän.

The pilot had served with the Kondor Legion in Spain, also fought in Poland, France and Norway. He had been with JG51 but on returning from leave he found he had been transferred to 1/JG77. The pilot had on him a certificate authorising him to use special ammunition, specified as explosive and incendiary.

Right: The cockpit interior of Hans-Jurgen Ehrig's Bf109 that force landed at Wagstaff Farm. Souvenir hunters have already liberated some instruments including the prized clock which was installed in the hole at the top of the panel next to the gunsight.

Below: Willy Fronhöfer's Bf109 at Jubilee Farm. The bullet hole in the engine cowling almost certainly contributed to his unscheduled arrival in England!

Above: Hans-Jurgen Ehrig's 'White 13' at Wagstaff Farm.

31 August 1940   **Bf109E-1**   **Wn.4448**   **4 +**   **1/JG77**   **MAP ID 12** (page 282)

Jenkins Farm, near Stapleford Abbotts, Essex. 13.15 hrs.

Attacked by two Spitfires during an escort sortie to Hornchurch aerodrome and the pilot crash landed the aircraft, hitting his head on the front of the cockpit. Numerous .303 strikes traced at the rear end of fuselage, cockpit cupola and both wings.
Markings: 4+, the spinner, cowling and wingtips of the aircraft were painted yellow.
Engine: DB 601, no. 30061.
Armament: four MG17. Standard armour plate bulkhead but no armour protecting the pilot.
ID: -, AW: -, FP: L 32066.
Ff: Ltn Jura Petrenko injured. (Has also been recorded as Bruno Petrenko)

The unit was assumed from the Feldpostnummer which was found on a letter dated 23rd August 1940. The pilot had a Russian father and a German mother but was of German nationality.

31 August 1940   **Bf109E-1**   **Wn.4068**   **8 +**   **1/JG77**   **MAP ID 13** (page 282)

Boxley, Kent. 13.20 hrs.

Took off from a Belgian airfield at 12.30 hrs for an escort operation to Hornchurch aerodrome, Essex. About twelve aircraft, flying at 22,000 ft in Vics-astern were attacked by fighters, this aircraft sustaining many hits, but the pilot managed to get away. Later he was again attacked and the control surfaces were so damaged that he had to bale out and his aircraft dived into the ground.
ID: 58201, AW: white, Köln, 3/4/40, FP: -.
Ff: Uffz Xaver Keck badly wounded.

Left: Uffz Xavier Keck.

The unit was deduced from the ID disc number. This was the pilot's first War Flight.

31 August 1940   **Bf109E-1**   **Wn.6092**   **5 +**   **1/JG77**   **MAP ID 14** (page 282)

Shornemead Fort, Gravesend, Kent. 13.20 hrs.

While escorting bombers at 23,000 ft to Hornchurch aerodrome this aircraft was attacked by a Hurricane, the controls and engine being damaged and the aircraft made a belly landing but started to burn and was almost completely destroyed.
Markings: most of the nose appeared to have been painted yellow.
ID: 58201, AW: white, Köln, 8/1/40, FP: -.
Ff: Fw Günther Kramer EKII badly burnt.

The pilot had in his pockets three receipts from shops in Aalborg dated 19th August 1940.

Left: Günther Kramer managed to force land his Bf109 successfully but the aircraft caught fire and burnt out within minutes.

Right: Another view of Günther Kramer's burnt out Messerschmitt.

MAP ID 15 (page 282)

31 August 1940	Bf109E-1	Wn.3652	9+	1/JG77

Hubble's Farm, Hunton, Kent. 13.25 hrs.

Shot down by a Spitfire and the pilot tried a forced landing at high speed but the engine was torn out and wings badly damaged.
Markings: 9 in white and stencilled on the tail 109.3652.
Armament: four MG17.
ID: 58201, AW: white, Köln Ostheim, 2/4/40, FP: L 32066.
Ff: Fw Walter Evers 58201/8 +. Maidstone, Kent.

The ID disc and Feldpostnummer were unidentified, along with Feldpostnummer L 14702 which was found on the parachute record booklet.

MAP ID 16 (page 282)

31 August 1940	Bf109E-1	Wn.4076		2/JG77

Elham Park Wood, Elham, Kent. 09.30 hrs.

While on a sortie with a number of other aircraft 'just to have a look around' a general dog-fight developed and the aircraft was shot through the engine by a Hurricane. The pilot baled out wounded from 5,000 ft, the aircraft caught fire, hit the ground and burnt out.
ID: 58202, AW: white paper on grey cloth, Köln Ostheim, 22/1/40, FP: L 03813.
Ff: Obltn Eckehart Priebe slightly wounded. Staffelkapitän.

The pilot was very reluctant to say anything under interrogation but without prompting he claimed he was with JG51.

Right: Obltn Eckehart Priebe photographed shortly before he was shot down over England.

Sandwich Flats, 200 yards from Princess Golf Club, Sandwich, Kent. 14.20 hrs.

About fifteen aircraft of II/KG3 started from Antwerp, at 13.00 hrs with an escort of Messerschmitt Bf109s to attack an aerodrome east of London, which they thought was Hornchurch. Having bombed their target, they were attacked by fighters and then they were fired at by a Vickers .303 gun which claims to have brought them down, although bullet strikes in the tail indicated fighter action. The pilot force landed the aircraft and the crew set light to it.

Markings: L in white.
Engines: Bramo Fafnir, nos. 14791 and 14375.
Armament: sixteen 50 kg bombs carried.
ID: 51591, AW: grey, Schweinfurt, 30/1/40, FP: L 18144.
Ff: Ofw Willi Lange wounded.
Bo: Uffz Fritz Krostopotsch wounded.
Bf: Fw Hubert Berndt wounded.
Bm: Fw Hans Wünsch wounded.

Left: An iconic image of the Battle of Britain showing 5K+LM on the Sandwich Flats. The crew performed a successful forced landing before setting fire to their aircraft.

Below: Two of the crew members are led away to captivity.

MAP ID 18 (page 282)

31 August 1940   **Do17Z-2**   **Wn.3264**   **5K+KM**   **4/KG3**

Above: The black 'jackdaw' emblem of II/KG3

300 yards north-west of Eastwick Farm, Burnham-on-Crouch, Essex. 13.25 hrs.

Eighteen aircraft, of II/KG3, started from Antwerp at 12.00 hrs to attack Hornchurch aerodrome. The course was over Gravelines, where they were met by a fighter escort of thirty to fifty Messerschmitt Bf109s. They flew across at 10,000 ft and claim to have bombed the objective, flying in Ketten Vic and dropping the bombs when the leader dropped. On the return, still in the Ketten Vic, they were attacked by about eight fighters and had to make a forced landing.

Shield: a black jackdaw on the branch of a tree, with white background. Spinners had white and red rings.

Armament: twenty 50 kg bombs carried.

ID: 51591, AW: grey, Schweinfurt, 13/1/40, FP: L 18144 Münster.

Ff: Ofw Alfons Bulach wounded.

Bo: Obltn Heinz Gahrtz sprained ankle.

Bf: Uffz Ernst-August Bock 51591/61 seriously wounded; died 3rd September 1940. CC 1/190.

Bm: Gefr Ernst Neumann unwounded.

MAP ID 19 (page 282)

31 August 1940   **Do17Z-3**   **Wn.3414**   **5K+GN**   **5/KG3**

At sea - near the Goodwin Sands, Kent. 14.00 hrs.

Started from a Belgian aerodrome at about 12.30 hrs with the objective to be Hornchurch aerodrome although the final choice was left to the formation leader and they dropped their bombs when he dropped his but did not know where this was. They were still maintaining formation along the Thames when they were attacked and with their ammunition nearly exhausted, both engines being hit, the aircraft crashed into the water from 12,000 ft.

Markings: G in white.

Armament: ten 50 kg bombs carried.

ID: 51592, AW: grey, Schweinfurt, 11/4/40, FP: L 18144.

Ff: Uffz Herbert Blasche EKII.

Bo: Fw Bruno Nickel EKII +. NKG.

Bf: Fw Emil Gudat EKII wounded.

Bm: Uffz Walter Sonntag EKII wounded.

MAP ID 20 (page 282)

31 August 1940   **Do17Z**   **Wn.3316**   **F1+BK**   **2/KG76**

Newchurch, near Dungeness, Kent. 18.05 hrs.

Having dropped their bombs the crew were making their way southwards between Maidstone and Canterbury, when they were attacked by about eight fighters which hit one engine and compelled the pilot to make a forced landing, but in doing so, badly damaged the aircraft.

Markings: B outlined in white, red spinners and red band round fuselage forward of the letter K. Shield: bomb falling on the British Lion.

ID: Bla 71043, AW: yellow, Gotha, 11/4/40, FP: -.

Ff: Ltn Josef Kleppmeier .

Bo: Fw Harald Pfaehler wounded.

Bf: Uffz Albert Bloss wounded.

Bm: Ofw Heinrich Lang wounded.

The unit was assumed from the ID disc and aircraft code.

Right: Dornier Do17Z F1+BK down at Newchurch.

| 31 August 1940 | Bf110C-4 | Wn.3617 | L1+ BK | 14(Z)/LG1 | MAP ID 21 (page 282) |

At sea - two miles north-north-west of Foreness, Isle of Thanet, Kent. 09.05 hrs.

This aircraft was flying last but one in the formation when the pilot became separated, was attacked by Spitfires, both engines and cockpit hit, the wireless operator being killed. Pilot brought the aircraft down on the sea as it was beginning to burn and got into his dinghy, subsequently being picked up.
ID: 53602, AW: Dienstelle L 08159 Paris, 22/8/40, signed Haupt. Kartel, Deputy Fliegerhorst Kommandant., FP: L 08159
Ff: Ltn Karl-Joachim Eichhorn. (Staffelführer)
Bf: Uffz Richard Growe +. NKG.

The pilot would not admit his unit but on a piece of paper it revealed that on 5th July 1940 he was authorised by Stabs Ingeneur Fleischhauer of Fliegerkorps VIII to pick up four Messerschmitt Bf110s in Romily for V(Z)/LG1.

| 31 August 1940 | Bf110D | Wn.3805 | L1+AK | 14(Z)/LG1 | MAP ID 22 (page 282) |

At sea - near The Nore Lightship, in the mouth of the Thames. 09.10 hrs.

This crew took off at 08.30 hrs on a free-lance patrol over the north side of the Thames. At 22,000 ft they were attacked from the rear by a fighter and as the aircraft could not maintain height, the pilot brought the aircraft down in the sea.
Markings: A in white.
AW: white, Fl.H.Kdtr.6/VI, 27/8/40, FP: -.
ID: Sch.Kp/Sch.FL. Ausb. Regt 10. & L.N.Fernsprech Ko.22.
Ff: Fw Gottlob Fritz EKII.
Bf: Ogefr Karl Döpfer, suspected to be suffering from pleurisy.

The pilot, aged twenty-one still had his pay-book on him which gave his movements since the outbreak of war:

2nd September 1939	Jagdfliegerschule, Werneuchen.
4th December 1939	Ergänzungs-Zerstörer Staffel 1.
27th March 1940	2/ZG 1.
11th May 1940	Ergänzungs-Zerstörer Staffel 1.
19th July 1940	14/LG1.
31st July 1940	Awarded Eiserne Kreuz II.
	V/Lehrgeschwader 1.

Air Intelligence initially deduced that the crew was from 2/LG1, from the aircraft markings given by the crew. It was later established that there was a fifth Gruppe, a Zerstörer unit using Messerschmitt Bf110 aircraft, the fourth letter being H, K or L and the colouring of the third letter, spinners etc. was white, red, or yellow respectively, the same as Gruppe I. Gruppe V could be distinguished by the fact that they use Messerschmitt Bf110s, whereas previous aircraft from Gruppe I, L1+ - H, K and L brought down were all Heinkel He111s and Junkers Ju88s. In addition Gruppe V had as a crest on their aircraft a Wolf's Head with a red tongue on a yellow background which had not been identified with aircraft of the other Gruppen.

| 31 August 1940 | Bf109E-7 | Wn.5600 | | 3/LG2 | MAP ID 23 (page 282) |

Chathill Park Farm, Crowhurst, Surrey. 18.45 hrs.

While on bomber escort duties, the pilot was severely wounded by numerous machine gun bullets and AA fire, his left foot was still in a surgical boot, as a result of a previous motoring accident, for which he had a press cutting on him.
ID: 53534, AW: -, FP: L 00931 Münster.
Ff: Obltn Hasso von Perthes EKI baled out severely wounded, died 14th September 1940. CC 5/330.

In spite of his wounds the pilot refused to give away any information.

MAP ID 24 (page 282)

31 August 1940	Bf110D-0	Wn.3396	3U+HS	8/ZG26

At sea - off Colne Point, East Mersea, Essex. 08.30 hrs.

Above: Obltn Hasso von Perthes poses with 'Brown 13' werke nr 1399. He died from wounds received after being shot down on 31st August over Crowhurst. Note the 3/LG2 Mickey Mouse emblem just behind his left hand.

Started at 07.00 hrs on escort duties. Attacked from the rear by three Spitfires, the rudder being completely shot away the crew baled out.

The wreckage of the aircraft was lying at the bottom of the river Colne Estuary. One Daimler Benz DB 601 engine found on land with red painted spinner and a petrol tank was recovered from the sea.

ID: 60042, AW: white, Krefeld, 13/1/40, FP: -.

Ff: Ltn Erich von Bergen.

Bf: Uffz Hans Becker.

A list of Motor Vehicles on the charge of 8/ZG26 was found on one of the crew.

Heavy automobile	Buick	5 seater	S.
Medium automobile	Mercedes	4 seater	S.
Medium automobile	Citroen	4 seater	U/S.
Motor Coach	Renault	25 seater	S.
Tender	Daimler	3.5 ton	S.
Tender	Renault	3 ton	S.
Heavy tender	Misse	4.5 ton	S.
Heavy tender	Leyland	5 ton	S.
Light van	Bedford	1 ton	S.
Motor-cycle	B.S.A.		U/S.
Motor-cycle	Matchless		U/S.
Trailer	Gauibschat	3.5 ton	S.
Trailer	Ackermann	3.5 ton	S.

South-East England, the Thames Estuary and the outskirts of London were again the chief scenes of air battles. The first raid started at about 11.00 hrs involving about 120 aircraft in a double attack. Damage and casualties were reported at Tilbury, Gravesend, Chatham and Gillingham but it appears the raiders were driven back from their intended targets. In a raid from 13.00 hrs to 14.00 hrs about 160 aircraft approached Biggin Hill and Kenley area, some enemy aircraft reached Croydon, but the second wave of this raid was driven back near the Kent Coast. At 15.30 hrs the Medway towns and aerodromes at Lympne and Hawkinge were under attack by bomb dropping Messerschmitt Bf109s. There was also considerable reconnaissance activity covering most of the British Isles during the day. Between 150 to 200 enemy aircraft were in action during the course of the night with bombing mainly being concentrated on the Bristol Channel area. Swansea and to a lesser degree Bristol were the places most heavily bombed. Enemy aircraft flying up and down the coast from Hull to the Wash were probably laying mines. It was noted that bombers appeared to be flying higher than normal with interceptions up to 20,000 ft.

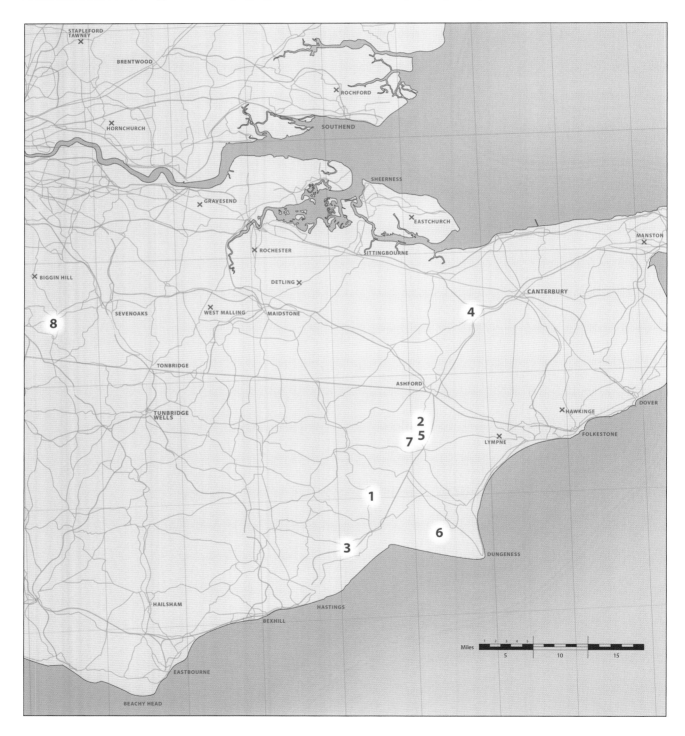

Newbridge, Iden, four miles north of Rye, Sussex. 14.03 hrs.

While engaged in a dog fight, this aircraft was hit in the engine, possibly by AA fire and the pilot made a good belly landing.
Markings: 11+I in white.
Armament: four MG17. It was reported that there were special gun cooling ducts on the engine cowling.
The top of Perspex hood was found to be thicker than normal.
ID: 60315, AW: -, FP: L 39570.
Ff: Ltn Josef Bürschgens EKI wounded.

A slip of paper found in the aircraft gave the wireless call signs for the 7th, 8th and 9th Staffeln indicating that the pilot was from III Gruppe, but he claimed he was from the 3rd Staffel, the ID disc and Feldpostnummer backing this assumption up.

It was subsequently reported that the aircraft was shot down by the rear gunner of a Messerschmitt Bf110 that the pilot had tried to formate on.

Burnt Oaks, Capel Farm, Orlestone, Kent. 10.30 hrs.

Above: Ltn Josef Bürschgens before and after being shot down near Rye.

Crashed following fighter action, the aircraft blew up and was completely destroyed and burnt out. The pilot baled out.
Armament and armour standard.
Ff: Ofw Paul Gerber +. CC 1/153.

Unit established from Ausweis.

1 September 1940   Bf109E-4   Wn.5087   10 + I   7/JG53   MAP ID 3 (page 298)

Winchelsea Bridge, Rye, Sussex. 12.00 hrs.

Started from Etaples at 10.45 hrs on a free-lance patrol, possibly with the intention of shooting balloons. The aircraft was attacked at 19,000 ft by a Hurricane from behind, the first burst damaged the engine. The pilot tried to maintain height and struggle home but he could not manage this and finally baled out at 1,500 ft. The aircraft crashed and burnt out.
Armament: two MG17 and two 20 mm cannon.
ID: 67401, AW -, FP: L 31005 Paris.
Ff: Ltn Herbert Strasser EKII.

The pilot's pay-book gave the following details:
1/9/39   Jagd Fliegerschule Schleissheim.
7/12/39   Ergänzungs Jagdgruppe, 2nd Staffel.
11/12/39 I/JG3.
28/12/39 Ergänzungs Jagdgruppe, 4th Staffel.
14/6/40   III/JG52, 7th Staffel.

MAP ID 4 (page 282)

1 September 1940   Bf109E-4   Wn.4020   9/JG53

Bush Field, Hurst Farm, Chilham, Kent. 17.00 hrs.

Following fighter action the pilot tried a high speed forced landing but the aircraft turned over and burnt out.
ID: -, AW: -, FP: -.
Ff: Obltn Oskar Bauer +. CC 1/167.

The pilot's pay-book gave the following details:
Fliegerausbildungsregiment.
15/12/39 Jagdfliegerschule.
10/8/40   9/JG53.
An unused picture postcard of Guernsey was also found on the pilot.

Above: Ltn Herbert Strasser sits on the mainwheel of his Bf109. The handle above his head is the hand starting crank which turned an intertia wheel, which in turn engaged the crankshaft when it reach a certain speed.

1 September 1940   Bf109E-4   Wn.1277   14 +   5/JG54   MAP ID 5 (page 298)

Haberdashers Wood, Ruckinge, near Bonnington, Ashford, Kent. 11.15 hrs.

Took off from an aerodrome in Belgium and while on escort duties flying towards the target, collided with another Messerschmitt Bf109 and the pilot baled out.
Markings: the whole of the nose of the aircraft was painted yellow.
ID: 71123, AW: -, FP: 36849.
Ff: Obltn Anton Stangl. Staffelkapitän.

1 September 1940   Do17Z   Wn.3369   F1+AT   9/KG76   MAP ID 6 (page 298)

Tarts Field, Lydd, near Dungeness Point, Kent. 16.00 hrs.

Took off from L'Ivry, north of Paris to bomb Gravesend aerodrome. On the return flight they were attacked by fighters which killed the wireless operator and both engines caught fire. Three of the crew baled out.
Markings: A and spinners in yellow. Black A on wings.
Engines: BMW 132.
ID: 51922, AW: yellow, Jessau, 27/2/40, FP: 23787.
Ff: Uffz Mathias Maasen wounded.
Bo: Ofw Wilhelm Illg.
Bf: Gefr Georg Spiess 71042/99 +. Folkestone, Kent.
Bm: Fw Heinrich Wöhner wounded.

Above: Dornier Do17Z F1+AT lies in Tarts Field at Lydd. At first glace the Dornier appears to have no swastika on the tail. However close inspection of the original print shows a faded swastika straddling the rudder hinge line in the early-war position.

The Air Ministry intelligence officer filled out the form (right) detailing the relevant information concerning the crashed aircraft and crew. This information was then used as a basis for the AI'g' and 'k' report. Pte Webb also produced the drawing below detailing the aircraft's markings.

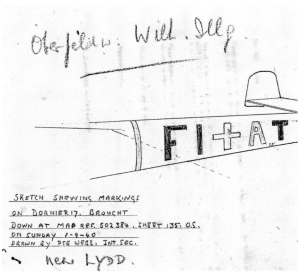

1) Date and time down: 1.9.40.   16.00.
2) Place down: *near the coast*
3) Aircraft type: Do. 17
4) Aircraft marks: *F1+AT* Staffel Colour: *Yellow*
5) Description of any Badge or Shield on aircraft: *don't know*
6) Unit to which crew belong: 9 Staffel. KG. 76
7) Feldpostnummer: 23787.
8) Ausweis (Colour, Place and Date of issue; Signature, if readable): *(a) yellow - Jever - 27.2.40. ohne Feldwebel 1.7.40 signed Roth 50 Kap. (b) Same - no promotion (c) Same*
9) Place of start: *won't tell*
10) Time of start (Our time): *won't tell*
11) Course, Height and Speed: *don't know*
12) Details of Combat: *attacked by fighters on way back Both engines on fire - baled out.*
13) Mission: *Bomb an aerodrome*
14) Number and Weight of bombs: *nil*
15) Result of Mission: *attacked objective*
16) Further attacks to be expected: ('Phone IMMEDIATELY to Fighter Command) *nil*
17) Morale and Reliability: *Morale good + fairly reliable*
18) CREW:

Function.	Rank.	Christian name(s).	Surname.	Identity Disc.	If wounded, etc.	Length of Service.
a)	Schf. Feldw.	Heinrich	Wöhner	51922/25	wounded	
b)	Fw. Ufz.	Mathias	Meassen	51922/57	wounded	
c)	Gef. Oberfeldw.	Will.	Illg	51922/11	not wounded	Nr 10
d)	Fw. Gefr.		Spiess			
e)						

19) Present Location and Telephone number of Survivors: *Benenden. Casualty Clearing Station -*

Oberfeldw: Will. Illg.

FI+AT

SKETCH SHEWING MARKINGS
ON DORNIER 17, BROUGHT
DOWN AT MAP REF. 502 384. SHEET 135T O.S.
ON SUNDAY 1-9-40
DRAWN BY PTE WEBB, INT. SEC.
~ near LYDD.

Tarpot Farm, Bilsington, Ham Street, south of Ashford, Kent. 14.00 hrs.

Started soon after mid-day to attack an aerodromes south of London with many other Messerschmitt Bf110s and Messerschmitt Bf109s crossing the coast unobserved in clouds they reached London before being spotted. This aircraft was attacked by a Spitfire which forced it to detach from the formation, shot up the starboard engine and damaged the intercom, the pilot diving down from 19,000 ft to 13,000 ft for some clouds but these disappeared over the Channel. Attacked again by three Spitfires and a Hurricane, the port engine was put out of action and the pilot turned for the coast and made a good belly landing.
Markings: O in white. Crest: Wolf's head in black picked out in yellow.
Armament: three MG17 (quoted in the AI1(g) report) and two 20 mm cannon found. No bombs carried.
ID: 53601, AW: grey, Würzburg, 21/7/40, FP: L 07206.
Ff: Ofw Rudolf Kobert EKI.
Bf: Fw Werner Meinig EKII.

Both airmen had served all through the French Campaign.

Below: A policeman and soldier inspect the ruptured earth caused by a German bomber trying to destroy the Messerschmitt Bf110 L1+OH which force landed at Tarpot Farm. The poles are anti-glider posts, erected in fields across southern England to discourage glider landings in the expected invasion.

Hosey Wood, one-and-a-half miles south of Brasted, Kent. 14.45 hrs.

Aircraft crashed and exploded; probably due to fighter action.
No identification markings traced.
Engines: DB601.
Ff: Fw Martin Jäckel +. CC 9/34.
Bf: Flieger Heinz Rösler +. CC 9/34.

South-East England and the Thames Estuary were again subjected to a series of attacks by enemy aircraft, using high level bombing in formation with heavy fighter escort, with about 750 to 850 aircraft being employed. The first attack was at 08.00 hrs but was turned away before their main objectives were reached. Some enemy aircraft reached London but no bombs fell there, the chief places being affected were Gravesend aerodrome, Rochester, Chatham, Maidstone and Tilbury. At 12.30 hrs there was a second attack in two waves, one from the direction of Dover and the second from the Thames Estuary with bombs again dropped on the same targets as the previous raid. At 16.00 hrs there was a double raid on the Biggin Hill area and Hornchurch, during which fighter patrols were maintained over the Straights of Dover. One formation reached Hornchurch consisting of thirty Dornier Do17s in close vics of five line astern, escorted by Messerschmitt Bf110s circling above and Messerschmitt Bf109s behind and above. Raiding was less intense than on previous nights with about 130 enemy aircraft in action. Most of the bombers followed the two, now almost customary, routes of Dieppe - Sussex - London to Birmingham and Cherbourg - Hampshire - Dorset - Gloucestershire and onto the Midlands. There were also some mine laying operations off the coast of Aberdeen. Minor bombing was reported in several places on the outskirts of London.

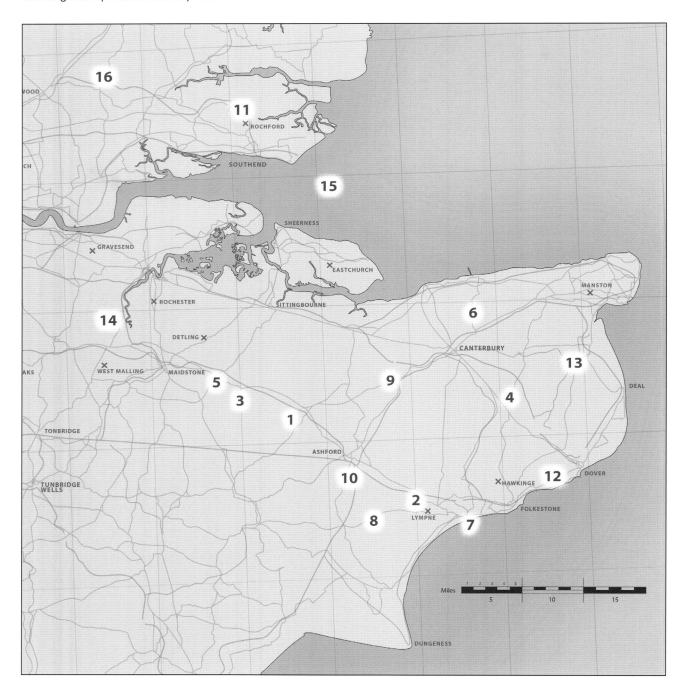

MAP ID I (page 304)

2 September 1940   Bf109E-1   Wn.6115   4/JG2

Cale Hill Park, Little Chart, near Charing, Kent. 13.13 hrs.

Above: The local souvenir hunters at Cale Hill Park get to work on Anton Glomb's 109. The expert in the foreground has chosen a suitably sized section to hide under the bed whereas the the two amateurs in the background may have more difficulty with their selected piece!

Crashed following fighter action and aircraft was totally destroyed.
Armament: four MG17 found in wreckage.
ID: 57002, AW: white, Zorbst, 22/1/40, FP: L 24155.
Ff: Uffz Anton Glomb EKII critically injured.

The unit was deduced from the ID disc and Ausweis. The place of start could not be ascertained, but shopping receipts showed that the pilot was at Bernay on 13th August 1940 and Rouen on 19th August 1940.
The pilot's pay-book gave the following details:
28/8/39   Flugzeugführerschule Magdeburg.
8/12/39   4/JG2.
30/4/40   6/JG2.
1/8/40   4/JG2.

He was awarded the Eiserne Kreuz II on 21st July 1940, the certificate being issued by Fliegerkorps V and signed by General von Greim.

A letter found on the pilot stated '... I was extremely sorry to hear that you had had such bad luck and it's a good thing it's all over. What luck that you managed to pull your aircraft up over the cliffs or the story might have had a different ending. Do you feel quite fit again, that you are flying again after such a short time? The Fatherland can be proud of its airmen; they've hardly got over one crash before they're off on another war flight'.

More photos of Anton Glomb's Bf109 after it crashed at Cale Hill Park. The wingtips appear to have been painted white. An MG17 lies in the foreground.

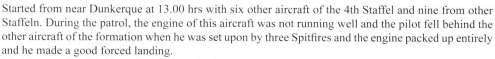

| 2 September 1940 | Bf109E-4 | Wn.1452 | 12 + - | 4/JG2 |

West Hythe, one mile south of Lympne Castle, Kent. 13.30 hrs.

Started from near Dunkerque at 13.00 hrs with six other aircraft of the 4th Staffel and nine from other Staffeln. During the patrol, the engine of this aircraft was not running well and the pilot fell behind the other aircraft of the formation when he was set upon by three Spitfires and the engine packed up entirely and he made a good forced landing.

Markings: -+12. Shield outlined in red with letter 'R' in red in centre.

Armament: two MG17 and two 20 mm cannon.

New type of material found to be used for self sealing petrol tanks.

ID: 67002, AW: -, FP: L 24115.

Ff: Uffz Emil von Stein slightly wounded.

The pilot's pay-book gave the following information:

1939   Fliegerausbildungsregiment 13, Neubiberg.

17/2/40   Jagdfliegerschule 3, Stolp.

17/5/40   3rd Staffel, Ergänzungsjagdgruppe.

14/6/40   II/JG Richthofen (2), 4th Staffel.

The pilot had made only one previous War Fight, over Portland and the Isle of Wight.

The Staffelkapitän of 4/JG2 was Leutnant Hahn.

Above: The famous JG2 'Richthofen emblem as carried by Emil von Stein's Bf109.

| 2 September 1940 | Bf109E-1 | Wn.3861 | | 9/JG2 |

Streets Farm, Ulcombe, six miles south-east of Maidstone, Kent. 13.10 hrs.

Aircraft shot down in fighter action, caught fire, dived into ground and buried in a large crater.

ID: -, AW: white, Dienststelle FPN 27317, 21/8/40, FP: 27315.

Ff: Ltn Werner Kluge tried to bale out but died in crash. All Saints, Ulcombe, Kent.

The pilot had in his possession a paper authorising him to go to the Dental Officer at the War Base Hospital, Le Havre and stamped Feldpostnummer 25371.

Right: The classic 'smoking hole' left by Werner Kluge's Bf109 at Streets Farm, Ulcombe.

| **2 September 1940** | **Bf109E-1** | **Wn.4807** | | **1/JG51** | **MAP ID 4** (page 304) |

Nethersole Farm, Womenswold, east of Barham, Kent. 08.00 hrs.

Aircraft crashed following fighter action and was completely smashed and burnt.
Armament: four MG17s were found amongst the wreckage but no armour plate was traced.

ID: -, AW:- , FP: -.
Ff: Ltn Günther Ruttkowski +. CC 1/36.

The pilot's pay-book gave the following details:
10/10/39 Schule Ausbildungsregiment 22, Pardubitz.
12/1/40 Jagdfliegerschule, Furth.
20/8/40 1/JG51.

| **2 September 1940** | **Bf109E-1** | **Wn.4850** | | **1/JG51** | **MAP ID 5** (page 304) |

Abbey Farm, near Leeds Castle, Kent. 08.00 hrs.

Aircraft caught fire in the air and the pilot baled out, the aircraft crashing in flames and completely wrecked.
The pilot claimed that he did not know what hit him but the aircraft just caught fire and he eventually baled out.
ID: -, AW: -, FP: -.
Ff: Ltn Helmut Thörl badly burned.

When interrogated, the pilot had no ID disc, Ausweis, or any documents, and initially refused to say a word. He had a few French coins in his pocket.

| **2 September 1940** | **Bf109E-4** | **Wn.1261** | **12 +** | **1/JG52** | **MAP ID 6** (page 304) |

Tile Lodge Farm, Hoath, near Westbere, Canterbury, Kent. 17.40 hrs.

Started at 17.00 hrs on a free-lance patrol with four other aircraft, developed engine trouble and while making a forced landing was attacked by a Hurricane. Crashed due to the engine being hit by 0.303 strikes. The port wing being torn off on landing.
Markings: 12 in white, along with the wing tips and tail tips. Upper and lower surfaces, aft half of rudder also white. Shield: Black boar on a white background.
Armament: two MG17 and two 20 mm cannon. Armour; standard bulkhead but nothing protecting the pilot.
ID: 65161, AW: white, Mannheim-Sandhofen, 2/2/40, FP: L 05612.
Ff: Fw Heinz Verlings EKII and Sudeten Medal.

The unit was deduced from the ID disc and the shield.

Below: A cropped version of this photo was used in the previous volume in relation to 'White 9' that crashed on 24th August. This newly found photo shows that one propeller blade of this aircraft was only slightly bent at the tip, thus ruling out this aircraft. The publishers therefore believe that this is actually White 12 that crashed at Tile Lodge Farm on 2nd September. Both aircraft appear to have received indentical damage to the port wing.

MAP ID 7 (page 304)

2 September 1940	Bf109E-1	Wn.3584	14 +	1/JG53

Small Arms School Ranges, west of Hythe, Kent. 08.17 hrs.

This pilot took off at 07.40 hrs on escort duties and made landfall at Folkestone, Kent in formation with the bombers flying inland, where a Spitfire cut him off from the others. As he was the last aircraft in the formation and finding himself isolated he made for home but a Spitfire chased him which after a complicated fight near the coast, shot into his petrol tank and he made a good forced landing.
Markings: 14 in white. Red circle around the fuselage.
Pilot's head armour showed 0.303 strikes but no penetration.
ID: 67005, AW: -, FP: 35821.
Ff: Uffz Werner Karl slightly wounded.

On previous occasions this airman had been involved in shooting down barrage balloons.

MAP ID 8 (page 304)

2 September 1940	Bf109E	Wn.6276	3/JG53

Bridge Farm, Bilsington, Kent. 08.50 hrs.

Shot down in combat, crashed in flames and completely burned out. No markings visible.
ID: 51575/2, AW: -, FP: -.
Ff: killed. Buried Aylesham Cemetery, Kent as an Unknown German Airman.
Now known to be Obltn Herbert Riegel. CC 5/152

MAP ID 9 (page 304)

Below: Obltn Ekkehard Schelcher of JG54.

2 September 1940	Bf109E-4	Wn.1574	Stab III/JG54

Mountain Street, Chilham, near Canterbury, Kent. 12.55 hrs.

Following fighter action, the aircraft dived into the ground and was completely destroyed.
ID: 51575, AW: -, FP: 24697.
Ff: Obltn Ekkehard Schelcher +. CC 8/168.

2 September 1940	Bf109E-1	Wn.3470	2 +	8/JG54

Finns Farm, Kingsnorth, near Ashford, Kent. 16.45 hrs.

The pilot was surprised by fighters, the aircraft engine being hit, stopped. The pilot force landed with wounds in his foot.
Markings: - 2 in black on fuselage just forward of windscreen. Camouflage; top of fuselage dark green, sides of fuselage mottle light green, lower surfaces light blue, with wing tips, tail tip and top of rudder painted white. Spinner three quarters white, one quarter black.
ID: 51577, AW: grey, München-Gladbach, 25/4/40, FP: L 24697.
Ff: Uffz Heinrich Elbers slightly wounded.

The ID disc and Feldpostnummer had been encountered before but not associated with a particular unit.

Below: Black 2 in a ditch at Finns Farm, note the white wing tips and tailplane tips.

MAP ID 10 (page 304)

Black 2 was recovered from Finns Farm and put on display to the public. This photo was taken in Blackpool. The narrow bordered fuselage cross was unusual for the period.

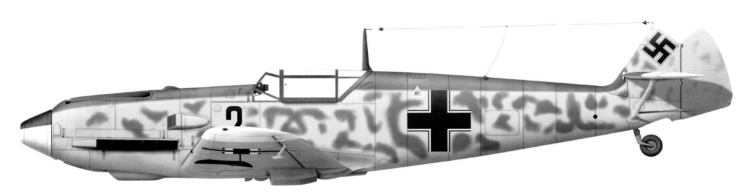

2 September 1940	Do17Z-2	Wn.3269	5K+BT	9/KG3

Rochford aerodrome, Essex. 09.15 hrs.

The crew took off from St. Omer to attack Eastchurch aerodrome, but were intercepted by fighters. On landing both engines were torn out and the fuselage was broken in two.
Markings: B in yellow. Crest on cowling, a red heart on a white square. Aircraft constructed by Henschel Flugzeugwerke.
Armament: seven MG15, along with two hand grenades.
ID: 51598, AW: grey, Würzburg; grey Schweinfurt, 31/7/40; grey, Würzburg, 16/2/40, FP: 38637.
Ff: Obltn Ullrich Rohr slightly wounded.
Bo: Fw Otto Sprink severely wounded.
Bf: Uffz Karl Seidel severely wounded.
Bm: Uffz Kurt Hilbrecht 51598/23 +. CC 1/369.

2 September 1940	Bf110C-4	Wn.3622	3M+HK	2/ZG2

Near St. Radigund's Abbey, West Hougham, Kent. 13.00 hrs.

Attacked by a Spitfire and the gunner baled out while the pilot force landed and then set fire to the aircraft.
Markings: H outlined in white,
Engines, DB601.
Armament: standard but no armour plate fitted.
ID: 53585, AW: -, FP: -.
Ff: Ltn Georg Schipper.
Bf: Gefr Theodor Schockenhoff.

Both of the crew refused to give any information to their interrogators but certain information was deduced from documents; this was:
On 2nd April 1940 the wireless operator was with I/Jagdfliegerschule, Stolp.
On 15th July 1940 both the pilot and wireless operator were ordered by Erganzungs ZG1 to fly KT+AF from Copenhagen to Neubrandenburg.
On 25th July 1940 both crew were ordered by Dienstelle Feldpostnummer L 32337 - Hamburg 1 (I/ZG 1) to report to the Truppensammelstelle (Personnel Collecting Point) of ZG 2 in Paris.

Below: Gefr Theodor Schockenhoff is escorted away after baling out of 3M+HK near Dover. His aircraft force landed near St Radigund's Abbey and was set on fire by the pilot, leaving little for the investigators. (right)

| 2 September 1940 | Bf 110D | Wn.3629 | A2+KL | 6/ZG2 | MAP ID 13 (page 304) |

Venson Farm, Eastry, Sandwich, Kent. 12.55 hrs.

Following fighter action this aircraft caught fire, crashed; the aircraft and its occupants being blown to pieces. A plate showed that the aircraft was manufactured by Focke Wulf, Bremen.
The wreckage of the aircraft was reported as taken by The London Scottish Regiment to Broom Park.
Ff: Fw Lorenz Beil 69024/8 +. CC 9/37.
Bf: Ogefr Johann Oehl +. CC 9/37.

The remains of two parachutes and a card bearing an airman's name were salvaged.

Left: The widely scattered remains of Bf110 A2+KL at Venson Farm.

| 2 September 1940 | Bf110D-1 | Wn.3309 | U8+DK | 2/ZG26 | MAP ID 14 (page 304) |

White Horse Wood, Birling, near Maidstone, Kent. 08.10 hrs.

Started from St. Omer at 11.00 hrs on a bomber escort mission. While flying at 16,000 ft this aircraft was attacked by four Spitfires, the whole raid being broken up and turned back, this aircraft was completely destroyed.
From a label found it showed that this aircraft was constructed by Focke Wulf, FZB, Bremen, with some parts supplied by Gothaer Waggonfabrik A.G.
ID: 60034, AW: grey, Crailsheim, FP: -.
Ff: Fw Karl Schütz 60034/9 +. CC 1/60.
Bf: Uffz Herbert Stüwe baled out wounded.

The unit of 1/ZG26 was deduced from the pilot's ID disc, while the wireless operator had a certificate issued at Güttersloh 2/KG54 on 23rd October 1939. The place of start was obtained from a late-leave pass issued to one of the airmen the previous night.

| 2 September 1940 | Bf110C-4 | Wn.3536 | 3U+GN | 5/ZG26 | MAP ID 15 (page 304) |

At sea - Thames Estuary, off the Nore Lightship, Kent. 09.00 hrs.

Started from St. Omer, at 08.00 hrs escorting bombers. The formation was flying at 19,000 ft westwards, up the Thames Estuary when this aircraft was engaged by fighters. During the dog fight the crew claimed to have shot down one Hurricane but the starboard engine was hit and a further attack stopped the port engine. The aircraft came down in the sea, and the crew took to their dinghy.
Shield; a wooden shoe.
ID: 60038, AW: grey, Werl, 29/1/40, FP: -.
Ff: Ofw Kurt Rochel EKII.
Bf: Uffz Willi Schöffler EKII.

Frith Farm, Laindon Road, Billericay, Essex. 1640 hrs.

Attacked by fighters the aircraft caught fire, crashed and burnt out.
Markings: D in white.
ID: 65140, AW: white, Jerver, 21/4/40 & grey, Dettingen, FP: -.
Ff: Olt Karl Wrede +. CC 1/371. Gruppe Technical Officer.
Bf: Uffz Richard Kukawka 65140/6 +. CC 1/373.

Right: The inverted wreckage of M8+DM at Frith Farm, note the white D outboard of the underwing cross.

3rd SEPTEMBER 1940

Just after 04.30 hrs two single raiders crossed over East Anglia, target unknown. Between 10.00 hrs and 11.30 hrs considerable numbers of enemy aircraft came in over North Foreland before dividing, part making for Essex and North Weald and part turning south over Maidstone, Manston and Hawkinge. Hawkinge was dive-bombed by Messerschmitt Bf109s which dropped six bombs and some delayed action ones. Manston was attacked by three unidentified aircraft. The heaviest attack was made on North Weald by twenty-five Dornier Do17s in a wedge shaped formation in vics of five, from 15,000 ft. They were escorted by fifty Messerschmitt Bf110s. The second attack was between 14.00 hrs and 16.00 hrs from Dungeness towards South London, bombs falling on Barnes and West Malling.

The numbers of enemy aircraft raiding Great Britain was again smaller than on previous nights. Including those aircraft engaged in mine laying operations in the Firth of Forth and on coastal operations from the Tyne to the Humber, no more than 100 aircraft were in action during the period. Raiding started at 21.00 hrs and quickly reached its peak when about forty aircraft were over the country at a time and then gradually diminished in intensity till the last few bombers turned for home at 03.30 hrs on 4th September.

Merseyside and the Bristol Channel were the principal targets with bombs also being dropped on Bournemouth and Southampton; probably by bombers returning to France from their raids on the North and Newcastle. In the earlier part of the evening bombs were dropped in Kent and Essex.

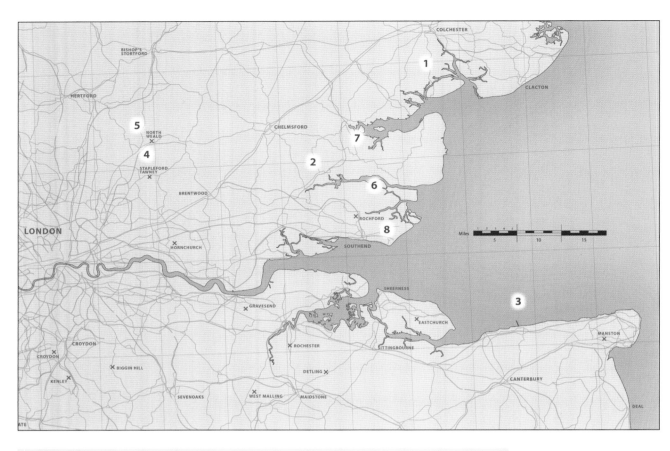

| **3 September 1940** | **Do17Z-2** | **Wn.3450** | **U5+AN** | **5/KG2** | **MAP ID 1** (page 314) |

Near Pyefleet Creek, Langenhoe, Essex. 10.30 hrs.

The whole of II/KG2, escorted by a mixed force of about twenty Messerschmitt Bf109s and Messerschmitt Bf110s were to attack North Weald aerodrome. The bombers were flying in Gruppenkeil formation (Gruppe, Staffel Vic, Ketten Vic astern) when they were intercepted by fighters and the pilot scuttled the bombs in an effort to escape. Aircraft was completely destroyed and buried twenty feet underground.

Armament: twenty 50 kg bombs carried.
ID: 58214, AW: grey, Fürth, 1/2/40, FP: L 00405.
Ff: Ltn Heinz Schildt +. NKG.
Bo: Fw Martin Kriegl.
Bf: Gefr Paul Niegisch +. NKG.
Bm: Uffz Emil Swindek +. NKG.

| **3 September 1940** | **Bf110C-4** | **Wn.3120** | **3M+CB** | **Stab I/ZG2** | **MAP ID 2** (page 314) |

Edwin's Hall, Woodham Ferrers, Essex. 11.00 hrs.

While flying at 19,000 ft on bomber escort duties, this aircraft was attacked by six Spitfires when the crew went to help another Messerschmitt Bf110 which was in trouble. Both crew baled out and the aircraft dived into the ground at high speed, both wings breaking off.

Markings: C in green; also a green C on wing tips. Four stripes on the tail of the aircraft Aircraft constructed by Gothaer W.F. at Gotha.
Engines: DB601.
No armour found, but standard armament.
ID: 55565 & 55566, AW: white, Köln, 13/1/40 & white, Garz/Pomm, 20/2/40, FP: L 06173.
Ff: Obltn Reinhold Messner. Gruppe Technical Offizier.
Bf: Ogefr Alois Santoni.

| MAP ID 3 (page 314) | 3 September 1940 | Bf110C-4 | Wn.2146 | 3M+BK | 2/ZG2 |

At sea - off Herne Bay, Kent. 10.45 hrs.

Started from a field near Paris, where there were only two aircraft and the crews lived in tents. While on a free-lance patrol, engaged at 13,000 ft by a Hurricane and one of the engines caught fire, so the crew baled out.

ID: 55565, AW: white, Köln, 12/1/40 & white, Gras, 20/2/40, FP: -.

Ff: Obltn Siegfried Gottschalt broken ankle. Staffelführer.

Bf: Uffz Max Hoffmann EKII.

The unit was assumed to be 2/ZG2 from the aircraft code as given by the crew and confirmed by ID disc number.*

*Actually believed to be a 1. Staffel crew flying a 2. Staffel machine.

Below: A flying boot was one of the few recognisable things left by the explosion of 3M+EK at Hobbs Cross.

| MAP ID 4 (page 314) | 3 September 1940 | Bf110C-4 | Wn.2065 | 3M+EK | 2/ZG2 |

Hobbs Cross, Harlow, Essex. 10.50 hrs.

Mid air collision with another Messerschmitt Bf110* and the crew baled out but neither parachutes opened properly; one appeared to have opened but must have got caught in the aircraft The aircraft crashed at high speed and exploded fifty minutes later and was completely burnt out and destroyed.

Aircraft constructed by Gothaer, W.F. Gotha Baumuster, BF110 C: dated 1939.

ID: 55565, AW: white, Köln, 13/1/40 & white, Garz/Jena, 20/2/40, FP: L 06173.

Ff: Fw Kurt Wagenbreth 55565/9 +. CC 5/323.

Bf: Uffz Aribert Schubart 55565/25 +. CC 5/322.

The unit was deduced from various papers and was confirmed by traces of red paint in the aircraft lettering and the ID disc. The pilot was at the Flugzeugführerschule C at Pütnitz on 25th April 1940.

*3M+HL Flown by Obltn Müller.

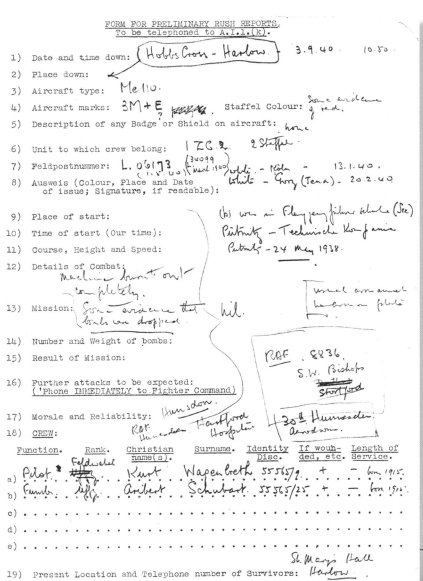

FORM FOR PRELIMINARY RUSH REPORTS.
To be telephoned to A.I.1.(k).

1) Date and time down: *Hobbs Cross – Harlow.* 3.9.40. 10.50.

2) Place down:

3) Aircraft type: *Me 110.*

4) Aircraft marks: *3M + E?* ~~~~. Staffel Colour: *Some evidence of red.*

5) Description of any Badge or Shield on aircraft: *none.*

6) Unit to which crew belong: *1 ZG 2. 2 Staffel*

7) Feldpostnummer: *L. 06173 (34099) (1.1.40) (1 March 1940)*

8) Ausweis (Colour, Place and Date of issue; Signature, if readable): *white – Köln – 13.1.40. White – Grny (Tena) – 20.2.40*

9) Place of start: *(b) was in Flyyyy film schule (See) Pütnitz – Technische Kompanie*

10) Time of start (Our time): *Pütnitz – 24 May 1938.*

11) Course, Height and Speed:

12) Details of Combat: *Machine burnt out completely.*

13) Mission: *Some evidence that bombs were dropped.* *hil.* *Usual armament + harm on plate.*

14) Number and Weight of bombs:

15) Result of Mission:

RAF 8836. S.W. Bishops ~~Stortford~~

16) Further attacks to be expected: ('Phone IMMEDIATELY to Fighter Command)

17) Morale and Reliability: *Hunsdon.*

18) CREW: *RAF Hunsdon. Hartford Hospital. 30th Hunsdon aerodrome.*

Function.	Rank.	Christian name(s).	Surname.	Identity Disc.	If wounded, etc.	Length of Service.
a) Pilot	Feldwebel	Kurt	Wapenbreth	55 565/9	+	— born 1915.
b) Funker	Uffz	Aribert	Schubart	55 565/25	+	— born 1915.
c)						
d)						
e)						

19) Present Location and Telephone number of Survivors: *St. Mary's Hall Harlow.*

Left: The original field report for the Hobbs Cross Bf110 showing the investigator's notes.
This report would be telephoned to Air Intelligence which in some cases led to mis-spellings and incorrect unit codes being transcribed.

Below: Another view of the Hobbs Cross Bf110 as soldiers pick through the pieces of wreckage.

Rye Hill, Thornwood, near Harlow, Essex. 10.50 hrs.

Started at about 10.00 hrs to escort bombers which they picked up on the French Coast. Flying above the bombers at about 24,000 ft, this crew collided with another Messerschmitt Bf110*, the collision smashing the port wing-tip and rudder, the pilot baling out, the wireless operator was probably hurt in the collision and did not get out. Aircraft burnt out on crashing, with only wing tips and tail left intact. Markings: H in yellow. Camouflage; dark green upper surfaces, light green on sides of fuselage, lower surfaces light blue-green. Seven vertical yellow stripes on rudder, four on a black background. Plate showed aircraft was manufactured by Gothaer FW Baumünster, BF110 C: dated 1940.
Engines: DB601 engines fitted, port engine marked Mercedes Benz gerat nr. DB 601 A, werke nr. 30711, constructed by Niedersachsische MW Braunschweig at Querum.
Armament standard. No armour plate found.
ID: -, AW: -, FP: L 06173.
Ff: Obltn Kurt Müller. Staffelkapitän.
Bf: Uffz Johannes Korn +. CC 5/213.

There were seven stripes on the tail of this aircraft, which was not the one usually flown by this crew as the previous day, they had been shot up and struggled home on one engine. The pilot claimed to have shot down two British aircraft.
The aircraft was a 3rd Staffel aircraft being flown by a crew from the 2nd Staffel.
*3M+EK Flown by Fw Kurt Wagenbreth

Below: Obltn Kurt Müller who baled out of his doomed Bf110 near Rye Hill. His pilotless aircraft came down reasonably intact as can be seen from the photos also below.

3 September 1940	Bf110C-4	Wn.3113	3M+EL	3/ZG2

Pudsey Hall Farm, Canewdon, Essex. 11.10 hrs.

Opposite page: More views of Obltn Kurt Müller's Bf110 3M+HL at Thornwood.

The crew starting from an airfield in the south-east of France, refuelled at an airfield on the Franco-Belgian frontier before flying across 'looking for trouble' and was engaged by three Spitfires from above. Both crew baled out and the aircraft dived into the ground and was buried at a depth of twenty feet.
Markings: Yellow wing tips and three yellow stripes on tail fin.
ID: 55566, AW: blue, Graz, 20/3/40 & white, Köln, 13/1/40, FP: 06173.
Ff: Ofw Gerhard Winkler slightly wounded,
Bf: Gefr Oscar Weiler.

The unit was assumed from the ID disc, Feldpostnummer and Ausweis as the crew refused to give their unit or aircraft code.

Right: And still the Bf110s fell. This is the starboard fin from 3M+EL which came down at Pudsey Hall Farm. The note in the report of 'yellow wingtips' is unusual for Bf110s of this period.

3 September 1940	Bf110C-4	Wn.3294	U8+KL	3/ZG26

At sea.

Attacked by fighters during an escort operation and the wireless operator baled out over the English Channel while the pilot forced landed the aircraft safely back at Fontend, France.
ID: 60035, AW: -, FP: 33440.
Ff: not named.
Bf: Uffz Horst Klatt 60035/17 +. CC 1/110. Washed ashore 13th September 1940, near Southend.
Orignally buried at Sutton Road cemetery.

3 September 1940	Bf 110 D	Wn.3310	3U+EP	6/ZG26

Maldon to Latchingdon Road, Mundon, two miles south of Maldon, Essex. 10.30 hrs.

Aircraft crashed following fighter action at low altitude after both engines were hit and disabled. Pilot's mirror and bullet proof windscreen were hit, causing it to look 'starred' but no penetration.
Markings: E in yellow. Shield; red and white curve sided diamond, with red diamond inside. Also a Dutch Clog painted yellow. Aircraft constructed by Gothaer W.F., BF 110 C dated 1939.
Fitted with DB 601 engines, starboard nr. 21226.
Armament: standard of five MG and two 20 mm cannon. No armour plate found.
Aircraft in good condition and was sent to the RAE.
ID: 60035 & 60039, AW: grey, Langendiebach, 9/3/40 & grey, Werl, 29/1/40, FP: -.
Ff: Ltn Walther Manhart.
Bf: Uffz Werner Drews severely wounded.

The crew refused to say a word during interrogation.

North Shoebury House, near Southend, Essex. 10.38 hrs.

Aircraft intercepted by fighters at 21,000 ft and shot down. The pilot was wounded in the head and shoulder from a rear attack.

Markings: K in white. Tail tips painted yellow with yellow stripes on outside of the rudders. Shield; penguin in black and white with a red umbrella. Spinners painted white.

Engines: DB601 N.1. port nr. 11937 and starboard nr. 11941. Manufactured by Mercedes Benz A.G. of 90 Berlin Marienfelde.

Armament: standard of four MG17, one MG15 and two 20 mm cannon. Bullet proof windscreen had been hit from behind but not penetrated. Semi circular armour bulkhead in front of pilot 11 mm thick and level with the pilot's chest. No armour plate behind the pilot's seat or behind rear gunner, both of whom were shot from behind.

ID: 60041, AW: white, Graz, 22/2/40, FP: -.

Ff: Fw Hans Grau EKII wounded.

Bf: Uffz Günther Uecker 60041/15 +. CC 1/109. Died of wounds 4th September 1940.

Air Intelligence found that they were unable to interrogate the pilot as he had become stone deaf due to shock. He had the certificate for the award of the Eisern-Kreuz II signed by Leutnant-General Lörzer of Fliegerkorp II.

The unit was assumed from the aircraft lettering, the ID disc not being known.

Below: Another Messerschmitt Bf110 with mention of yellow tactical markings. This time described as 'tail tips painted yellow'. Despite being wounded in the head and shoulder, the pilot, Hans Grau, managed to perform a very good forced landing at North Shoebury House.

During the day enemy aircraft carried out two raids, the first was between 09.15 hrs and 10.15 hrs when bombs were dropped on Eastchurch, Lympne and Bradwell-on-Sea aerodromes, along with a few other places in Kent and Essex. The second raid was between 13.00 hrs and 14.15 hrs and was a double thrust, the first via Shoreham to Weybridge and Brooklands and the second via Dungeness to Rochester, Eastchurch and Rochford. Dover barrage balloons were again attacked. Bombs were dropped on Eastchurch, Lympne, Brooklands, Shoreham, Rochester airport and Rochford, incidents of a serious nature were at the Vickers Armstrongs works at Weybridge, Surrey and Pobjoy's Factory at Rochester, Kent. The attack on Brooklands and Weybridge areas was made by Messerschmitt Bf110s which dive bombed, while other bombers flew at 10,000 to 13,000 ft. Raiding for the night started shortly before 21.00 hrs and lasted until about 04.30 hrs 5th September, when between 150 to 200 aircraft were in action over the country. Minor bombing was reported from some districts of London. There was a sustained attack on Liverpool, Sleaford, Tilbury, Stoke on Trent, Bournemouth and Bristol. There were also bombs dropped on Kent, Sussex, Gloucestershire and Somerset.

It is noted that daylight pattern bombing from high levels was again employed and that the success of this form of attack depends on the skill of its leaders, and that the other crews who are both junior in rank and less experienced. Their instructions were to simply fly close and release their bombs when told. Frequently they may not even know their objective, therefore a successful attack on the leader should seriously jeopardize the remainder.

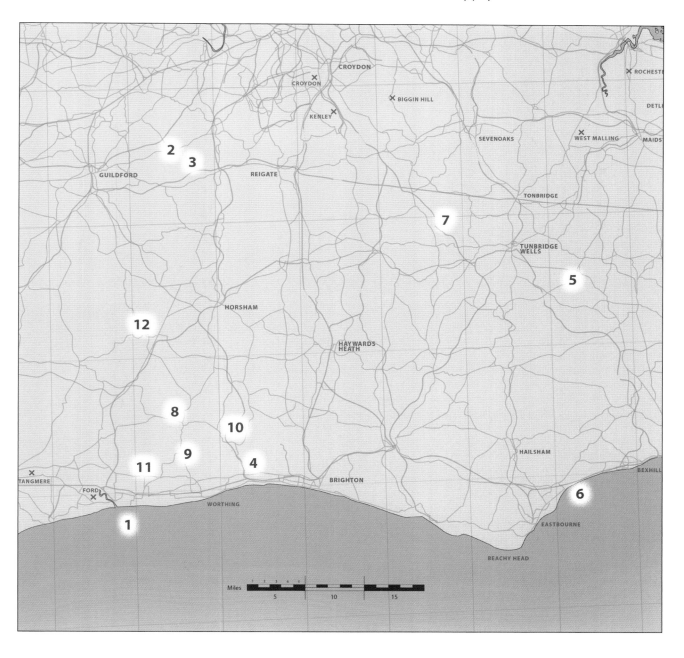

| 4 September 1940 | Bf110D-0 | Wn.3390 | S9+AB | Stab EproGr 210 | MAP ID 1 (page 321) |

At sea - off Littlehampton, Sussex. 13.25 hrs.

Failed to return from operations over Britain due to unknown causes.
Ff: Hptm Hans von Boltenstern +. NKG. Gruppenkommandeur.
Bf: Fw Fritz Schneider 53602/7 +. CC 4/46. Picked up by a boat and initially buried at Newhaven.

Took off from Calais-Marck to attack Brooklands. Unaccountably von Boltenstern dived straight into the Channel without a shot being fired.

| 4 September 1940 | Bf110D | Wn.3303 | L1+BK | 14(Z)/LG1 | MAP ID 2 (page 321) |

Long Reach, West Horsley, Surrey. 13.45 hrs.

While on a free-lance patrol consisting of twelve Messerschmitt Bf110s covering the Brooklands Raid, they were returning home, when they were attacked by a Hurricane. The wireless operator baled out at 12,000 ft, fairly seriously wounded. The pilot was still in the aircraft when it crashed, the wreckage lying in a large crater.
Shield: Wolf's head.
ID: -, AW: blue/grey, Mannheim, April 40, FP: L 08159 Paris.
Ff: Fw Karl-Arthur Röhring +. Brookwood, Surrey.
Bf: Uffz Joachim Jäckel wounded.

| 4 September 1940 | Bf110D | Wn.3306 | L1+FK | 14(Z)/LG1 | MAP ID 3 (page 321) |

Green Dene, West Horsley, Surrey. 13.45 hrs.

Dived into the ground following fighter action and burnt out.
Markings: 3 in yellow on wing-tip. F on outside of wing cross. Shield; a green heart with white edges, with Belgian and French flags painted on it.
ID: 53602, AW: blue/grey, Würzburg, 30/1/40, FP: -.
Ff: Obltn Michel Junge +. Brookwood, Surrey. Staffelkapitän.
Bf: Uffz Karl Bremser 53602/13 +. Brookwood, Surrey.

The crew was identified by a prisoner as being members of 14/LG1, the ID disc and Feldpostnummer confirming this.

| 4 September 1940 | Bf110C-4 | Wn.2116 | 3M+AA | Stab ZG2 | MAP ID 4 (page 321) |

Mill Hill, Shoreham-by-Sea, Sussex. 13.50 hrs.

Took off at 12.35 hrs. Attacked by five Spitfires, the port engine stopped and as things were getting fairly hot for them, the crew made a good forced landing. This aircraft was also claimed by a Blenheim crew from Martlesham Heath.
Markings: Spinners: red ring, S on each side of the cockpit, Lebens Gefahr (danger to life) in red on each side of the nose. Badge; a horizontal red lightning flash.
Engines: DB601. A number of .303 strikes in each engines indicated that both had cut out.
Armament standard. Armour: a semi circular plate 10 mm thick behind four staggered MG17s, 29 inches x 17 inches radius. 1 foot in front of this and just behind the ammunition boxes there was another piece of armour plate 8 mm thick 29 inches across and 15 inches radius and pilot's windscreen protected with bullet proof glass 2½ inches thick.
ID: 30035, AW: grey, Werl, 30/1/40 & grey, Crailsheim, 15/1/40, FP: 37026.
Ff: Obltn Wilhelm Schäfer. Geschwader Adjutant.
Bf: Uffz Heinz Bendjus slightly wounded.

Above: Obltn Wilhelm Schäfer.

The unit was wrongly assumed by Air Intelligence to be Stab ZG76 from the aircraft markings. The wireless operator's disc had previously been identified as 1/ZG26.

On 23rd August, the pilot had been shot down off Portland in a Messerschmitt Bf110, his wireless operator was killed and he was wounded in the shoulder. He took to the rubber dinghy, threw out the bag of orange dye and was eventually picked up by an aircraft from the Seenotdienst.

Opposite page: Looking like a badly made Airfix kit, 3M+AA lies on Mill Hill near Shoreham-on-Sea. The horizontal red lightning flash mentioned in the report can just be discerned on the nose of the aircraft.

Little Butts Farm, Cousley Wood, near Wadhurst, Sussex. 13.35 hrs.

Started from Le Mans at 14.00 hrs on an escort sortie. Flying at 16,000 ft they were attacked by a number of Spitfires from behind, the pilot making a particularly good forced landing.

Markings: A and spinners in green. Shield: red serpent on a white background underneath the front part of the fuselage. Airframe card gave date of manufacture as 11th April 1940 by MIAG Muhlenbau und Industrie A-G, Braunschweig, manufacturer's markings TD+GD.

Engines DB601, nos. 64599 and 65121 manufactured by Daimler Benz, Genshagen on 4th June 1940 and 6th June 1940.

ID: 65142, AW: white, Nellingen, 10/1/40 & red, Langendiebach, 24/4/40, FP: 33333 Frankfurt.

Ff: Obltn Hermann Wieber EKII, Spanish and Four Years Service Medals.*

Bf: Uffz Max Michael wounded.

Further details about the Messerschmitt Bf110 were also found:

Petrol tanks 4. Total capacity 1,270 litres.

Oil tanks 2. Total capacity 70 litres.

Speed in horizontal flight at ground level 475 kph.

Speed gliding or diving 700 kph.

Maximum flying weight 6950 kg.

Maximum landing weight 6750 kg.

* *Pilot Obltn Hermann Wieber was the Gruppenadjutant of Stab, II./ZG 76.*

Below: An unexpected visitor!
One can only imagine the reaction of the Brissendens as this shark mouthed Messerschmitt careered up the hill and ended up in their garden.

The investigator's interpretation of the shark's mouth as a 'red serpent on a white background' is interesting!

SUSSEX CONSTABULARY REPORT

I have to report that at 13.35 hours on the 4th September, 1940, an enemy Messerschmitt 110 aeroplane crashed in the garden of Little Butts Farm, Cousley Wood, occupied by Mr R T Brissenden. There were two occupants in the machine namely Lieutenant Hermann Wieber, the pilot, no.33333, Sergeant Max Michael, the gunner, no. 36736. The gunner was injured having two bullet wounds in the chest and one in the throat, the pilot was uninjured. The plane was damaged but was not on fire. The military were the first to arrive on the scene and they had taken charge of the two prisoners. The uninjured pilot was taken to the headquarters of the 5th Loyal North Lancashire Regiment, stationed at Wadhurst Castle, telephone Wadhurst 177. The injured gunner, after receiving attention from Dr.Roberts of Wadhurst, was taken to the Kent and Sussex Hospital, Tunbridge Wells, in the Tunbridge Wells Police ambulance. I notified Biggin Hill, RAF Station, of the crashed aircraft and the whereabouts of the two prisoners. A military guard was placed on the machine by the 5th Loyal North Lancashire Regiment. All prisoners' property, maps etc, were taken charge of by the 5th Loyal North Lancashire regiment and I understand were taken to their headquarters at Wadhurst Castle.

| 4 September 1940 | Bf110C | Wn.3287 | M8+IM | 5/ZG76 | MAP ID 6 (page 321) |

At sea - seven miles off Pevensey Bay, Sussex. 13.45 hrs.

Started from Abbeville at 13.00 hrs on a free-lance patrol some distance to the west of the main attack. The whole Staffel flew at 15,000 ft, making landfall between Eastbourne and Bexhill, while the bomber formation made landfall approximately over Dungeness on the way to London. The Staffel were attacked by several Spitfires and Hurricanes when near London and this aircraft had both engines damaged. The pilot struggled to get home but had to make a forced landing in the sea. They got out the rubber dinghy and started to row towards France, but realising this was hopeless, gave it up and turned back.
The pilot was the Gruppe Adjutant.
ID: 53585, AW: grey, E 103, 22/1/40 & grey, Schleissheim, 8/2/40, FP: L 33333.
Ff: Obltn Freiherr Ernst Hartmann von Schlotheim EKI.
Bf: Uffz Georg Hommel wounded.

This crew claimed to have shot down six British aircraft.

| 4 September 1940 | Bf110C | Wn.2089 | M8+CP | 6/ZG76 | MAP ID 7 (page 321) |

Saxbys Farm, Cowden Pound, Edenbridge, Kent. 13.23 hrs.

Shot down by fighters and blown to pieces.
Markings: G and spinners in yellow and also a 3 on the wing tip. Shield; a green heart with white edges, Belgian and French flags painted on.
Engines: DB601.
ID: 62748 & 62682, AW: dark blue, Oldenburg, 16/4/40, FP: L 36068 & L 30264.
Ff: Obltn Günther Piduhn 62748/3 +. Tonbridge, Kent.
Bf: Uffz Rudolf Condne 62692/78 +. Tonbridge, Kent.

The pilot's ID disc was that of 4/KG30 and the Feldpostnummer of ZKG30 and also had in his possession a wireless certificate issued by I/KG30 on 1st July 1940. The wireless operator had no papers but his ID disc was for 7/KG27.

| 4 September 1940 | Bf110C-1 | Wn.2837 | 2N+DP | Stab III/ZG76 | MAP ID 8 (page 321) |

Church Farm, Washington, West Sussex. 13.20 hrs.

Probably shot down by fighters the aircraft dived into a field from great height in flames and was totally destroyed; it was not possible to obtain any information as the aircraft was lying in a crater twenty feet deep. Flames from the burning aircraft lit up the position of No. 461 Battery, R.A. during the raid.
ID: 53565, AW: green, Fliegerhorstkommandantur E 106, 22/7/40, signed Leitner, FP: -.
Ff: Obltn Helmut Florenz +. NKG. Staffelführer.
Bf: Gefr Rudi Herbert +. NKG.

From the Sussex Constabulary Report: The machine that fell at Washington was seen to fly over from the North-West at some 6,000 ft chased by a Hurricane. Several bursts of gun fire rang out over the Downs and the Messerschmitt burst into flames and nosed down, striking the ground at high speed and exploding. All that was left was a blazing crater in a field just west of Church Farm.

| 4 September 1940 | Bf110C-4 | Wn.3254 | 2N+BM | Stab III/ZG76 | MAP ID 9 (page 321) |

Honeysuckle Lane, High Salvington, Sussex. 13.25 hrs.

Started at 13.00 hrs on escort duties from Abbeville. Crashed following fighter action, the crew having baled out and aircraft was totally burnt out.
Markings: B in white, also on wings, with white rings round spinners.
Engines: DB601, one plate showed werke nr. 63441.
Armament: no guns or armour found.
ID: 69009, AW: -, FP: 00722.
Ff: Obltn Walter Schiller. Staffelführer.
Bf: Fw Helmut Winkler wounded.

The crew was very unresponsive during interrogation and hardly answered yes or no to questions. The unit was wrongly deduced by Air Intelligence from the aircraft lettering and ID disc to be 4/ZG 1.

Below: Yet another Messerschmitt Bf110, this time 2N+BM that fell at Honeysuckle Lane. A remarkable total of 12 Bf110s crashed within a 30 minute period on 4th September in the Sussex area, making a total of 20 Bf110s lost over England within 48 hours. Further 110s were lost at sea or crash landed back in France.

| 4 September 1940 | Bf110C-4 | Wn.3563 | 2N+HM | 7/ZG76 | MAP ID 10 (page 321) |

Strivens Farm, Steyning, Sussex. 13.30 hrs.

Started from an aerodrome near Laon on escort duties. There were about twenty-five Messerschmitt Bf110s in all escorting a bomber formation which flew direct to Portsmouth at 20,000 ft. This aircraft became separated and on being attacked by fighters, forced landed with its undercarriage retracted.
Markings: H in white. Three yellow wasps with white wings painted on the nose. Stencilled on a fin was 3563. White rings on spinners. Four circles with the following dates on both fins; 12th August 1940, 13th August 1940, 15th August 1940, 1st September 1940.
Standard DB601 engines. No armour plate found.
ID: 69010, AW: white, Westerland, 2/2/40, FP: L 01894.
Ff: Uffz Wilhelm Schultis.
Bf: Uffz Richard Bileck very badly wounded.

The unit was identified from the aircraft code, wasp insignia, ID disc and Feldpostnummer.

Below: Ltn Hans Münich, (second left), with fellow POWs in Canada. Münich was the pilot of 2N+CN which crash landed at Black Patch Hill. Second from right (tallest of the 5) is Obltn Wilhelm Schäfer, Geschwaderadjutant of ZG 2 and pilot of 3M+AA, shot down on 4th September 1940.

| 4 September 1940 | Bf110C-4 | Wn.3101 | 2N+CN | 8/ZG76 | MAP ID 11 (page 321) |

Blackpatch Hill, Patching, four miles north-east of Angmering, Sussex. 13.45 hrs.

Took off from Abbeville aerodrome. While on escort duties, before reaching their objective this aircraft was attacked by a Spitfire from below and was not seen by the crew. The right engine caught fire and the pilot made a forced landing. The aircraft caught fire two minutes later and was burnt out.
Markings: C in black, outlined in white. Spinners red. Badge; three wasps on fuselage. No armour plate found.
ID: 53585 & 69010, AW: white with grey back, Neuburg, 12/5/40 & white, Gütersloh, 10/4/40, FP: L 32337 & L 01402.
Ff: Ltn Hans Münich.
Bf: Uffz Adolf Käser.

The unit was assumed from the aircraft lettering and the three wasp badge. The pilot's ID disc had been encountered with various units and his Feldpostnummer showed that he was recently with Ergänzungszerstörerstaffel 1 and that until 19th July 1940 he was in Schlessheim. The gunner was from 7/ZG76.

Below: The three wasp emblem carried by 2N+CN was painted directly onto the fuselage camouflage as seen on this example.

Above: Hans Münich's burnt out 2N+CN on Blackpatch Hill.

Right: John Peskett's notes for this aircraft.

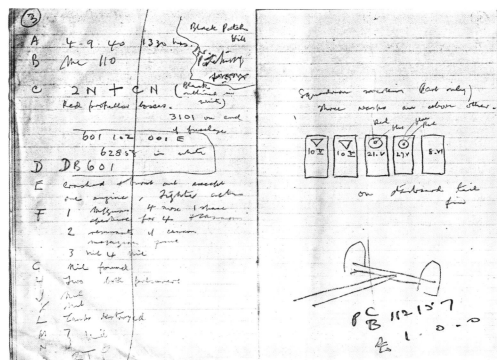

| MAP ID 12 (page 321) | 4 September 1940 | Bf110C-4 | Wn.2104 | 2N+KP | 9/ZG76 |

Toat Farm, Wisborough Green, Sussex. 13.20 hrs.

Took off from Abbeville aerodrome. Shot down due to fighter action and crashed in flames inverted. The aircraft and crew were smashed to pieces and although three feet were found, only the pilot could be initially identified.
No guns or armour found.
FF: Obltn Kurt Raetsch 53585/30 +. CC 9/53.
Bf: Ogefr Werner Hempel +. CC 9/53.

Crew originally buried in St.Mary's Churchyard, Pulborough.
Date of manufacture of starboard engine 21st October 1937 and on the starboard engine 23rd October 1939.

Left: The remains of the crew of 2N+KP were initially laid to rest in Pulborough cemetery.

Once again raids were made on two separate occasions with bombs being dropped in the South-East of England. The first raid lasted from about 09.40 hrs to 10.40 hrs, involving 170 aircraft and saw bombs dropped in some eastern suburbs of London and parts of Kent, including Biggin Hill. The second raid, which lasted from about 15.00 hrs to 16.30 hrs included attacks on oil tanks at Thameshaven and on Detling aerodrome by about 200 to 300 aircraft. The tactics adopted by the enemy during the second raid were:

At 15.00 hrs 150 aircraft in three formations came in between Deal and Dover, one of which turned back after two minutes. The other two formations carried on to Canterbury where they split, the larger one of 100 aircraft went to Biggin Hill, while the smaller formation of fifteen aircraft went north-west across the Estuary. Here the smaller formation was joined by a fourth formation of twenty aircraft flying direct from France via Ramsgate, and they proceeded to attack Thameshaven and return down the estuary together. The Biggin Hill formation turned back and flew out via Maidstone and Rochester. While these operations were going on, a fifth formation of about six bombers, escorted by twenty Messerschmitt Bf109s came straight in for Detling, which it bombed and then went straight back.

It was estimated that about 100 enemy aircraft took part in the night's raiding with bombs being dropped in smaller quantities than usual except in London and Liverpool. In each of these places the main damage was to railway communications.

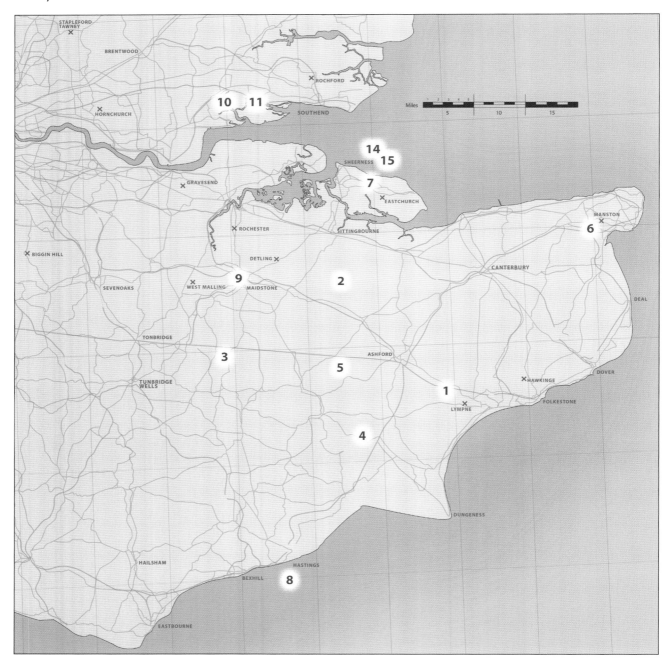

Banks Farm, Aldington, Kent. 10.10 hrs.

Started at 08.40 hrs escorting Dorniers that were attacking Croydon. On return from the attack some Spitfires and a Hurricane split this aircraft off from the formation and shot into the engine. The pilot made a good forced landing but engine mounting broke off at the bulkhead. About fifteen .303 strikes were spread over the fuselage.

Markings: 6 in white, outlined in black. Rudder and wing tips white. Shield: a white worm outlined in black, with a red tongue. Two vertical stripes on rudder. Plate identifies aircraft as constructed by Erla NW werke nr. 1985 dated 23rd June 1940.

Armament: two MG17 under engine cowling, two wing cannon guns, one marked 20.02 mm and the other 20.04 mm. Under the latter is 'Warning' MG F.F. 'M'. Standard 8 mm bulkhead armour plate but no head protection for pilot.

ID: -, AW: white on blue card, Köln, 22/1/40, FP: L 28083.

Ff: Ltn Heinz Schnabel EKII, slightly wounded.

The worm on the fuselage was the badge of I/JG3, the first Staffel using white, the 2nd red and the 3rd yellow.

The two stripes on the tail were scored by the previous pilot. Prior to the war the pilot was a Civilian flying instructor and was called up into the German Air Force at the outbreak of war. Operational experience as escort on raids over Portland, Eastchurch and Manchester* were amongst his fifteen War Flights. During the French Campaign the pilot was wounded at Lille.

* Clearly beyond the range of even the most ambitious Bf109 pilot! Probably a transcription error.

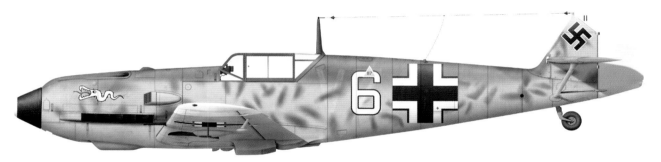

Below: Rural English life goes on around White 6 which force landed at Banks Farm on 5th September.

More views of White 6 at Banks Farm. The white wingtips have been covered with earth to make them less conspicuous from the air. The aircraft appears to have overpainted factory codes visible on the fuselage.

The pilot Heinz Schnabel was later to become involved in an audacious escape attempt when he and another German pilot escaped from their POW camp and stole a Miles Magister from nearby RAF Carlisle. Unfortunately for them, they had insufficient fuel to complete their escape and reluctantly landed back into captivity near Great Yarmouth.

5 September 1940	Bf109E-4	Wn.750	7 +	3/JG3	MAP ID 2 (page 330)

Wichling, Kent. 10.30 hrs.

Started from near Boulogne, acting as escort for ten Dornier Do17s. The pilot had just made a small circle above the bombers when he was suddenly attacked by a fighter, which he did not see. With his engine hit, he made a forced landing.

Markings: 7 in yellow and yellow tipped spinner, followed by white and green segments. White tips to wings and rudder. Crest; white serpent with red tongue. Camouflage; fuselage mottled dark and light green and grey wings. Airframe built by Erla nr.750, 1938.

Engine: DB601 A/1 nr. 30674 made by Henschel Cassel.

ID: 55570, AW: white, 22/7/40, FP: L 03045 Münster II.

Ff: Uffz Heinz Grabow badly wounded.

The pilot had only spent three weeks with his present Geschwader as previously he had been acting as an escort for Red Cross aircraft. The whole of JG3 were based at Boulogne.

Below: An Australian photo of Yellow 7 that force landed at Wichling. The airframe was despatched to Australia as a recruiting tool for the RAAF. It appears to have gained a different rudder in transit as the report mentions white paint applied to the wing tips and rudder.

5 September 1940	Bf109E-4	Wn.1480	< + -	Stab II/JG3	MAP ID 3 (page 330)

Winchet Hill, Love's Farm, near Marden, Kent. 10.10 hrs.

Force landed following fighter action, in good condition. Starboard wing showed many .303 strikes. Markings black outlined in white. Crest; U shaped, outlined in red, divided into eight segments, coloured black and white. Wing tips and rudder painted white. Camouflage: all blue. Spinner divided into alternate black and white sectors.

Engine: DB601 A, made by Mercedes Benz werke nr. 10598.

Armament: two MG17 and two 20 mm cannon.

ID: 57009, AW: grey, Zerbst (Anhalt), 26/3/40, FP: -.

Ff: Obltn Franz von Werra EKI.

The pilot was Adjutant of the Gruppe, his ID disc number being three below that of 6/JG3. According to other PoWs from the Gruppe, this pilot gave a talk on German Radio describing an attack on an aerodrome near Rochester, on about the 26th August, when he shot down four Hurricanes which were about to land, set fire to a hangar and riddled five more Hurricanes on the ground. When confronted by the text he strenuously denied the broadcast, although regarded by fellow officers as a 'Hell of a Fellow' and kept a pet lion cub.

Below: Von Werra with his pet lion cub Simba.

One of the most famous downed Bf109s of the Battle of Britain, Franz von Werra's E-4 that came down on Winchet Hill. Von Werra was immortalised in the film 'The One That Got Away' which told the story of his successful escape from captivity.

More views of von Werra's 109, in the view (left) it appears that someone has cleaned the oil off the unit emblem seen above.

| 5 September 1940 | Bf109E-1 | Wn.3627 | 2 + - | 5/JG27 | MAP ID 4 (page 330) |

One mile east of Appledore Station, Kent. 16.50 hrs.

Crashed following fighter action, dived into the ground, buried in a deep crater and burnt out.
Markings: Plate; BFW.109 302 Regensburg 3836/12.
Fitted with DB601 engine.
Ff: Obltn Helmut Strobl 53537/4 +. The pilot's remains were located on 5th September 1986 when the aircraft was excavated. He was finally laid to rest in the family plot at Kolbnitz, Austria.

| 5 September 1940 | Bf109E-4 | Wn.1949 | | 1/JG52 | MAP ID 5 (page 330) |

Bethersden, near Ashford, Kent. 10.30 hrs.

Shot down in combat with British fighters and dived into the ground.
Airframe made by Erla. Completely broken up.
ID: 65161, AW: L 07141, 22/8/40, FP: -.
Ff: Uffz Eugen Kind 65761/14 +. CC 1/175.

Monkton Farm, near Manston, Kent. 15.45 hrs.

Below: 51 year old Wilhelm Meyerweissflog put his Bf109 down in a field near Manston after being shot down on his highly individual patrol!

This pilot set out on a very free-lance patrol. The pilot of this aircraft was born on 27th October 1889, learned to drive a car in 1911 and was an observer in the German Air Force during the First World War. After the war he was a reservist and lived at Zurich with a Technical Bureau and when called up, he became an Admin Officer attached to the staff of JG3. He had recently been on leave, returning late on the evening of 4th September, he thought, to a place near to Boulogne. On the next day, shortly after lunch, looking out of his window, he saw a lot of the boys going off and thought he would like a flip too so he jumped into his Messerschmitt, flew vaguely in the direction of England and was neatly shot through the fuel tank by a British fighter and made a forced landing, from which, by more luck than good judgement, he came out safely. When apprehended, he had not the slightest idea where he was.

A number of .303 strikes in the oil cooler caused the engine to overheat and fail.

Engine: DB601 A/1, Mercedes Benz nr. 62783 dated 13th August 1940.

Camouflage: light navy grey, red band twelve inches broad round engine cowling. Half red, half white spinner, white wing tips and rudder.

ID: 67003, AW: grey, Dienststelle FPN L 24846 Frankfurt-am-Main 23/7/40, FP: -.

Ff: Hptm Wilhelm Meyerweissflog.

The red stripe on the nose was applied to replace the unit's 'Ace of Spades' emblem, apparently ordered by Goering as a punishment.
In retaliation, many pilots painted out their swastikas as seen on page 348.

| 5 September 1940 | Bf109E-1 | Wn.4017 | 7/JG53 | MAP ID 7 (page 330) |

Rayhams Farm, Eastchurch, Kent. 16.30 hrs.

Following fighter action the aircraft crashed and was completely burnt out.
Markings: white wing tips and red spinner,
Armament: two MG17 and two 20 mm cannon found amongst the wreckage. Armour; standard bulkhead and head piece for pilot 8 mm thick.
Ff: Ltn Joachim Deutsch +. NKG.

| 5 September 1940 | Bf109E-1 | Wn.6252 | 9/JG53 | MAP ID 8 (page 330) |

At sea - twelve miles off Hastings, Sussex. 15.30 hrs.

Believed to have been shot down in combat and forced landed on the sea.
ID: 6404, AW: grey, 12/2/40, FP: 25656.
Ff: Fw Anton Ochsenkühn.

The pilot would give no information about his mission or how he was brought down; his unit being established from a flight order dated 3rd August 1940, headed III/JG53. The ID disc was that of the 9th Staffel.

Left: The smoking remains of Fritz Hotzelmann's Bf109 embedded in number 6 Hardy Street, Maidstone. Note the back of the exposed fireplace in the upstairs room.

5 September 1940	Bf109E-4	Wn.1096	+ 6	1/JG54

Above: Fritz Hotzelmann.

Right and below: The chimney sweep emblem of 1/JG54. Probably not the best sweep to have gone through the fireplaces at number 6 Hardy Street!

No. 6, Hardy Street, Maidstone, Kent. 11.15 hrs.

Started from a field aerodrome fifteen miles south of Calais at 10.20 hrs. The whole Gruppe started from the same aerodrome and flew at 19,000 ft to the side of the course used by the bomber formation. They had no connection with the bombers as escort but were to cause a diversion. This aircraft became engaged in a dog fight over Biggin Hill and the engine was damaged. The pilot tried to escape and was followed for some distance by a Spitfire; the engine eventually failing when near Maidstone. The pilot baled out; the plane being a complete wreck.

Markings: top of rudder and tail planes painted white. Shield: a chimney sweep carrying a ladder; an emblem only used by aircraft of 1/JG54.

ID: 69018, AW: white, Böblingen, 10/1/40, FP: L 35620.

Ff: Uffz Fritz Hotzelmann.

The pilot refused to give his unit during interrogation but enquired after a Leutnant Held who belonged to Stab I/JG54. The pilot also enquired after Oberfeldwebel Otto Schöttle who was from the same Staffel, thus the unit could be confirmed by ID disc, Ausweis and Feldpostnummer. The pilot was on his fifteenth War Flight, amounting to about one every other day.

The pilot's career was established as follows:

24th December 1938	Issued with pilot's certificate by Flugzeugführerschule, Görlitz.
March 1940	Flying Training School, Herzogenaurach.
May - July 1940	Ergänzungsjagdgeschwader 21. Known as the 'Erzatz Staffel'.

5 September 1940	Bf109E-4	Wn.5291		Stab III/JG54

Little Chalvedon Hall, Bowers Gifford, Essex. 15.20 hrs.

Shot down by fighters, the aircraft broke up in the air and was smashed to pieces. The pilot baled out but his chute failed to open.

Markings: + B painted out. Spinner white. Crest; two 109s on an oval in black and white. Badge; an aeroplane between two horizontal bars.

ID: -, AW: grey, Köln Ostheim, 22/1/40, FP: -.

Ff: Hptm Fritz Ultsch +. CC 1/370.

5 September 1940	Bf109E-4	Wn.5284		9/JG54

South Benfleet, Essex. 15.20 hrs.

Believed to have been shot down in combat with fighters and the pilot baled out. The pilot's parachute failed and his body was not found until 17th September 1940.

Ff: Fw Heinrich Dettmer 51578/6 +. CC 1/456.

5 September 1940   He111H-3   Wn.3324   V4+AB   Stab I/KG 1 (Hindenburg)

Rendlesham, near Eyke, Suffolk. 01.10 hrs.

Started from Northern France to bomb Tilbury. Just before reaching the objective, when flying about 16,000 ft, the aircraft was caught in searchlights and well held. The pilot turned northwards and snaked downwards, trying to avoid the lights but could not escape. A Blenheim from Martlesham got on their tail and stopped the port engine, the bomb load being scuttled. They then partly escaped the searchlights but were very quickly picked up again and with half the crew wounded, flying at 1,000 ft they decided to bale out. The pilot actually jumped and made a good landing from 650 ft.

The underside of the aircraft was lamp-blacked, including the German cross on the side and Swastika on the tail, but in spite of this it was held very well in the searchlights.

Engines: Jumo 211 D. Starboard engine no. 3853, port engine no. 38535.

Armament: uncertain as it had been removed to RAF Station Martlesham. Three stick grenades found.

ID: 53550 & 53553, AW: grey/white, Koppel, 6/3/40 & 8/3/40, FP: -.

Major Ludwig Maier 53553/1 +. CC 1/224. Gruppenkommandeur.

Ff: Obltn Hans-Dietrich Biebrach.

Bo: Obltn Job-Wilhelm G von Rittberg 53550/6 +. CC 1/313. Baled out but his chute failed.

Bf: Ofw Erwin Stockert 53553/10 +. CC 1/220.

Bm: Uffz Horst Bendig +. CC 1/223.

The pilot who was a reservist called up at the outbreak of war, used to be a pilot with Lufthansa, flying on the Croydon and Manchester routes. The crew had been together throughout the war, taking part in the Polish and French Campaigns. This was also the third time they had been shot down, once for each campaign.

Left and below: The remains of V4+AB at Rendlesham, note how the national markings have been roughly overpainted with black distemper to reduce visibility for night operations.

5 September 1940	He111P	Wn.3065	5J+JP	6/KG4

Suffolk Street, Sunderland. 23.18 hrs.

Attacking Newcastle or Sunderland this aircraft received a direct hit by AA fire, crashed and caught fire in the town of Sunderland, causing civilian casualties. From a pencil sketch found in the aircraft it was deduced that the target may have been Newcastle.

Armament: only one MG15 and half standard armoured bulkhead recovered.

Mrs Rachel Stormont, 55, Suffolk Street, Sunderland +.

ID: 55538, AW: green, Fliegerhorstkommandantur E22/XI, 9/7/40, FP: L 06885 Hamburg 1.

Obltn Hans-Werner Schröder 55538/83 +. Hylton, Sunderland.

Uffz Franz Reitz 55538/59 +. Hylton, Sunderland.

Ogefr Rudolf Marten +. Hylton, Sunderland.

Ogefr Josef Wich 55538/77 +. Hylton, Sunderland.

Below: The remains of 5J+JP in Suffolk Street, Sunderland. Two battered MG15s lie in the foreground.

The unit was identified from the ID disc number and Feldpostnummer, along with the wireless operator's certificate dated 19th July 1940. On a scrap of paper was the marking He 111 TD+OZ.

MAP ID 14 (page 330)

5 September 1940	He111 H-2	Wn.2632	A1+GR	7/KG53

At sea - The Nore, off Sheerness, Kent. 15.30 hrs.

During bombing operations to attack the oil depot at Thameshaven attacked by fighters and seen to crash into the sea.

ID: 69042, AW: grey, FP: 03171.

Fw Hermann Bohn 69042/24 +. CC 1/415. Washed up Reculver, east of Herne Bay, Kent on 3rd October 1940.

Uffz K Bickel +. NKG.

Uffz F Bolz +. NKG.

Uffz F Rosenberger +. NKG.

Gefr K Haak +. NKG.

The ID disc was that of 7/KG53 and was confirmed by the Feldpostnummer. The format of the Ausweis and traces of signature also indicated the unit.

At sea - The Nore, off Sheerness, Kent. 15.30 hrs.

Started at 13.15 hrs to bomb the oil tanks at Thameshaven. The mission was accomplished and the aircraft was shot down by AA fire on the return flight. The aircraft sank and three of the crew drowned, two of the crew being rescued by a patrol boat. The prisoners revealed that this was their third attack on Thameshaven in three days, the two previous attacks were driven off; the whole of the Gruppe taking part in each attack.

Armament: eight bombs of an unknown size were carried in each attack.

ID: 69042, AW: grey, Giebelstadt, 1/2/40, FP: L 03171.

Ff: Fw Anton Maier.

Bo: Fw Irwin Agler +. NKG.

Bf: Uffz Heinz Lenger wounded.

Bm: Uffz Rudolf Armbruster +. NKG.

Bs: Gefr A Nowotny +. NKG.

The unit and aircraft code was assumed from the ID disc, Ausweis and Feldpostnummer.

GERMAN AIR FORCE TRAINING, EXPERIENCE AND MORALE.

During the latter part of August 1940 it was noticed that many airmen captured were inexperienced in war conditions with many of the older hands being sent back to Germany. One rear gunner, although having served in the Air Force for some time had done very little gunnery training and received no practice at all from an aircraft. The average age of a pilot was twenty-four with four years service; that of an observer was twenty-eight and four years service; that of a wireless operator twenty-two and three years service and that of a gunner nineteen and one year service.

It was noted by the Medical Officer examining prisoners: 'during the past ten days Prisoners of War show definite evidence of nervous exhaustion. All reflexes are +++, pupils are widely dilated and there are marked tremors and motor restlessness'.

German aircraft carried out three raids on Great Britain, the first from 08.30 hrs to 10.00 hrs involving 250 aircraft in five formations, came in between Romney and Ramsgate, spread out fan wise to Hornchurch, Chatham, Kenley, Tunbridge Wells, Brighton and Hailsham areas. The second from 12.45 hrs to 14.00 hrs by 200 aircraft in four formations to Maidstone and the Thames Estuary, during which a number of bombs were dropped. There appeared to be an offensive patrol of Messerschmitt Bf109s which split into several different formations, going up to Hornchurch in the north and Redhill in the south. The third raid involved 150 aircraft between 17.30 hrs to 19.00 hrs flying over the Thames Estuary and was made up of Messerschmitt Bf109s at 10,000 ft aiming for Thameshaven.

In the other raids, Junkers Ju88s and Dornier Do17s were employed at 15,000 to 20,000 ft, with escorts close behind at only 500 feet higher. Messerschmitt Bf109 offensive patrols were reported by pilots at 20,000 to 25,000 feet; one formation was encountered at 31,000 feet. The Southern Railway lines to Caterham and Oxted were blocked temporarily and very slight damage was done to the Hawker Hurricane aircraft factory at Weybridge and at Pobjoy's Factory at Rochester. During the night operations were less extensive, the main objectives being London and Liverpool, with the oil installations at Thameshaven being bombed. Reconnaissance operations continued west of Eire and went up as far as the Shetlands.

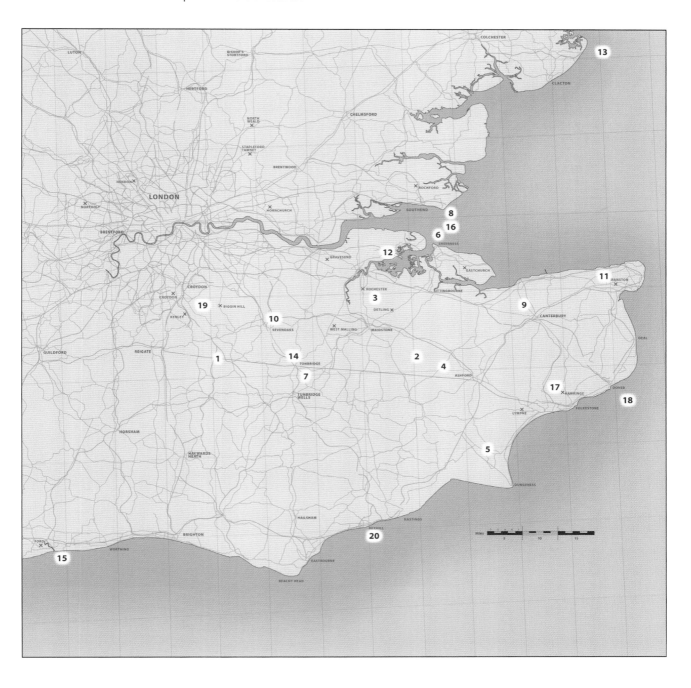

6 September 1940	Body Recovered			

At sea - Portland, Dorset.

The body of a German airman was washed ashore having been in the water for a considerable time.
ID: 62793, AW: yellow, Köln, 13/3/40, FP:-.
Fw Hummel EKII +. NKG.
The name was deduced from a Postal Order counterfoil stamped 'Bonn-Hangelar 19/7/40' and from rank badges.

6 September 1940	Bf110D-0	Wn.3373	S9+BH	1/ErproGr 210

MAP ID 1 (page 343)

Flow Meadow, Foyle Farm, Crowhurst, Surrey. 09.15 hrs.

Started from Valenciennes at 08.30 hrs landing at Calais-Marck and starting again at 09.10 hrs for an attack on Weybridge, Surrey with seven other aircraft. This aircraft was attacked by three Hurricanes and turning for home was shot down. The aircraft exploded on hitting the ground and was buried in a deep crater.
Markings: B in red*. Plate showed aircraft was constructed by MIAG.
Armament: two 20 mm cannon and one MG15 found. Reported to have been carrying two SC 500 kg bombs.
ID: 53581, AW: red, Köln, 22/7/40, FP: L 17172 LGP Münster, 18/8/40.
Ff: Uffz Gerhard Rüger +. NKG.
Bf: Gefr Edmund Ernst baled out.
Details of the raid were found on a piece of paper in the Kommodore's aircraft that was shot down on 27th September. This aircraft had previously attacked Vickers on the 4th September and on this raid had taken a course from Calais to Cap Griz Nez where it had climbed for fourteen minutes, assembling the escort before heading off towards Kenley where they turned for Weybridge; the return route was a direct course for Boulogne.
*Post-war research by John Vasco shows that the letter B was in blue.

Above: Uffz Gerhard Rüger.
Below: S9+BH, the aircraft in which Rüger died on 6 September.

6 September 1940	Bf109E-4	Wn.5044	< +	Stab JG2

MAP ID 2 (page 343)

Plumtree Farm, Headcorn, Kent. 09.00 hrs.

Started at 08.00 hrs on a preliminary patrol before the arrival of the bombers. Intercepted at 650 ft by two Spitfires, the pilot baled out but badly broke his thigh on landing. Aircraft dived into ground and was completely burnt out, only part of wing and the tail left.
ID: 53521, AW: Grey, Würzburg, 13/2/40, FP: L 14015.
Ff: Ltn Max Himmelheber badly injured.
The pilot was too badly injured to be interrogated, his unit being assumed from his ID disc, Feldpostnummer and Ausweis. A plate found in the aircraft with 3277 was presumed to be the werke nummer.

6 September 1940	Bf109E-4		2 + ~	8/JG2

MAP ID 3 (page 343)

Bleakwood, Walderslade, near Chatham, Kent. 14.30 hrs.

Started from Boulogne at 13.00 hrs on an escort mission. During preliminary interrogation this pilot stated that about 200 Messerschmitt Bf109s were escorting bombers. This aircraft collided with another at a height of 21,000 ft before reaching the objective, and crashed with its tail broken off.
Markings: 2 in black. White cowling and red band round spinner.
Engine DB601.
Armament: Two shell guns marked 'Achtung FFM'.
ID; 53518, AW: white, FP: L 26603.
Ff: Obltn Karl-Heinz Metz EKII, Four Years Service Medal and Sudeten Medal.
The pilot proved uncommunicative during interrogation and was carrying no papers.

MAP ID 4 (page 343) | **6 September 1940** | **Bf109E-4** | **Wn.2781** | **1 + I** | **7/JG26**

Hothfield, Kent. 09.20 hrs.

While escorting bombers on a raid to Kenley aerodrome, attacked by a fighter and made a good forced landing, after which the pilot set fire to the aircraft which was burnt out.
ID: 60315, AW: white, Dortmund, 15/1/40, FP: -.
Ff: Ltn Hans Markwart Christinnecke wounded.

The unit was assumed from the ID disc and Ausweis as the pilot refused to give any details.

MAP ID 5 (page 343) | **6 September 1940** | **Bf109E-1** | **Wn.3877** | **5+ I** | **7/JG26**

Swamp Farm, Old Romney, Kent. 10.40 hrs.

Cause of crash unknown. Aircraft burnt out after crashing.
Markings: I in white. Whitewash on wing tips and rudder.
Armament: four MG17. No head armour for pilot.
Ff: Gefr Karl Gustav Holzapfel +. Folkestone (New) Cemetery.

In an horrific incident, it seems that the pilot crash-landed his aircraft and was trapped in its cockpit as fire took hold. A group of soldiers arrived on the scene only to see the pilot being burned alive; he was shot dead to prevent further suffering. When the flames were extinguished it proved impossible to identify the man, who was buried as 'Unknown' the Folkestone (New) Cemetery.
Research by the historian Joe Potter has lead to this being accepted as the grave of Karl Gustav Holzapfel.

MAP ID 6 (page 343) | **6 September 1940** | **Bf109E-1** | **Wn.3225** | **11+** | **3/JG27**

At sea - Nore Boom, off Sheerness, Kent. 18.15 hrs.

Started at 17.30 hrs in formation with more than one hundred Messerschmitt Bf109s on escort duties. The aircraft met the bombers off the French coast and escorted them to the attack on Thameshaven. This aircraft was shot down by a Spitfire on the return journey.
Markings: 11 in yellow.
ID: 2 St. I 77, AW: -, FP: L 39553.
Ff: Obltn Werner Schüller wounded.

Although this airman had the old style ID disc which showed that he belonged to 2/JG 77, he claimed that he belonged to 3/JG27 and the Feldpostnummer confirmed this.

MAP ID 7 (page 343) | **6 September 1940** | **Bf109E-4** | **Wn.2762** | **6 + -** | **5/JG27**

Bank Farm, Tudeley, near Tonbridge, Kent. 09.20 hrs.

Left from a field aerodrome near St. Omer at 08.30 hrs. Course St. Omer – Griz Nez – London at a height of 15,000 ft, escorting a smaller number of bombers, which were picked up over Griz Nez. At 15,000 ft they were attacked by a Spitfire from behind and sustained hits in one wing and engine. The coolant ran out of the engine and the pilot turned and tried to get home but was followed by a Spitfire, so he jumped out.
Markings: 6 in black, with white edges, horizontal bar in red.
Armament: one 20 mm cannon and two MG17 found.
ID: 53537, AW: white, L 25704, 28/8/40, FP: L 25704.
Ff: Fw Erich Braun slightly wounded.

The pilot freely gave his unit but his ID disc was one number below that of 7/JG52. He had often made two sorties per day but usually had two rest days off per week.

MAP ID 8 (page 343) | **6 September 1940** | **Bf109E** | **Wn.1380** | | **Stab III/JG27**

At sea - Shoeburyness Artillery Range Buoy, Essex. 18.02 hrs.

While escorting bombers, which were attacking the oil tanks at Thameshaven, an engine defect developed and the pilot turned for home. Attacked by fighters and caught fire; the pilot baled out badly burned.
Badge; a black cross with brown edging, three aeroplanes in brown on the horizontal arm of the cross.
ID: 51515, AW: blue, Handorf, 21/1/40, FP: -.
Ff: Hptm Joachim-Heinrich Schlichting injured. Gruppenkommandeur.

Blean, near Canterbury, Kent. 18.45 hrs.

Started at 18.15 hrs from an aerodrome on the French Coast approximately six miles west of Calais, on a patrol. The aircraft was flying with the whole of the 7th Staffel, at 15,000 ft when it was attacked and shot in the radiator by Hurricanes.

Markings: Engine cowling white, with a white 8 on a grey rectangular background. Balkenkreuz on fuselage. Badge: a red cross on black ground with a gold aeroplane.

Engine: DB 601 A/1, built 29th August 1940.

Usual bulkhead armour but no pilot's head shield. Fuselage made by Gerherdt Fiesler Werke Cassel.

ID: 51516, AW: red, Fürth,15/5/40, FP: L 00369 Frankfurt.

Ff: Uffz Ernst Nittmann.

The pilot prior to 25th June 1940 had been with 6/JG27 had been wounded on a previous War Flight over England in August 1940 as a result of which he was in hospital for fourteen days.
It was also revealed that an Unteroffizier Ackmann, also of 7/JG27 crashed at some point off the English Coast and was missing. (26/8/40).

White 8 caused quite a bit of interest when it was put on display in Cornwall. The unusual position of the aircraft number on the cowling was a feature common to III Gruppe aircraft in JG27. The description of the emblem is confusing as it would normally be a black cross on a white background.

Stone Street, near Sevenoaks, Kent. 11.30 hrs.

Started at 10.00 hrs from an aerodrome near the French Coast on bomber escort duties. This aircraft was shot down by Spitfires from a height of 21,000 ft before reaching the objective. The pilot baled out but proved to be uncommunicative during interrogation.
Airframe made by Erla, in 1939.
ID: 65163, AW: white, Mannheim-Sandhofen, 2/2/40, FP: L 18969.
Ff: Obltn Heinrich Waller.

As the pilot was uncommunicative the unit was assumed by Air Intelligence from the ID disc to be 3/JG52, while the Ausweis had been encountered with 1/JG52.

Vincent's Farm, Manston, Kent. 18.50 hrs.

Started at 17.30 hrs on a free-lance patrol. This aircraft was flying with four others from the same Staffel at a height of 16,500 ft when it was shot down by fighters. The pilot tried to land at Manston aerodrome but undershot and crashed. One wing buckled but otherwise in fair condition.
Markings: 5+I in white. White spinner, cowling and rudder. Thick red band round cowling, painted out. Camouflage; mottled light and dark green and grey. Aircraft manufactured by Erla werke nr.1506 / 1940.
Engine: DB601 A/1, manufactured by Mercedes Benz werke nr. 62611.
ID: Jagdfliegerschule, Schleissheim, AW: grey, Wiesbaden, 12/2/40 FP: L 31005.
Ff: Uffz Hans Georg Schulte EKI.
The pilot during his interrogation gave his unit as 7/JG53, which he had been with since May 1940 but his Feldpostnummer had been encountered with 7/JG52.

White 5 was another 109 that appeared in the UK with white tactical markings around this time. The controversial JG53 red nose band had been obscured by the white paint but was still noticeable to the investigator. He didn't however make any mention of the missing swastika on the tail. The swastika had been overpainted apparently in protest over the imposition of the red band in place of the unit's 'Ace of Spades' emblem.

MAP ID 12 (page 343) **6 September 1940** **Bf109E-4** **Wn.1129** **8/JG53**

Kingsnorth Marshes, River Medway, Kent. 18.00 hrs.

Shot down by fighters and aircraft partially broke up in the air. Aircraft under water and only visible at low tide. Only the pilot's body was recovered.
ID: 67402, AW: -, FP: L 31925.
Ff: Fw Ernst Hempel 67402/12 +. CC 1/350.

The unit was assumed to be 8/JG52 from the ID disc, the number being one above that of 7/JG52. The pilot's certificate was found, issued from Fliegerausbildungsregiment 52, Halberstadt, 14th February 1939.

MAP ID 13 (page 343) **6 September 1940** **He111H-3** **Wn.6912** **A1+AB** **Stab I/KG53**

At sea - off Harwich, Essex. 18.00 hrs.

Started from an aerodrome in northern France at 16.30 hrs with a mission stated to be weather reconnaissance over East Anglia. At 16,000 ft the aircraft was attacked by four or five Spitfires and dived to escape but both engines were hit and the pilot put the aircraft down on the sea. The crew got out and inflated the rubber dinghy, but two of the crew drowned while doing this.
Markings: B in white.
ID: 69037, AW: grey, Ostheim, 18/7/40, FP: -.
Ff: Ofw Martin Winter.
Bo: Obltn Albin Weber.
Bf: Ofw Gerhard Müller +. NKG.
Bm: Gefr Hohnisch +. NKG.
Bs: Fw Fiedrich Kempgens EKII, Sudeten, Austrian and Four Years Service Medals.

The ID disc was two numbers below that of 3/KG53 and the white B, the only letter on the fuselage visible, made Air Intelligence believe that the aircraft was A1+BH.

MAP ID 14 (page 343) **6 September 1940** **Ju88A** **Wn.8104** **F1+HP** **6/KG76**

Tanyards Farm, Tonbridge, Kent. 09.15 hrs.

Started from a field aerodrome in the Calais / St. Omer area at about 08.15 hrs, flying towards London. On crossing the coast near Hastings, Sussex, the aircraft was hit by AA fire in the left wing but continued on towards the objective believed to have been Kenley aerodrome. They were next attacked by fighters from behind, which shot into the right engine that later caught fire. The flight engineer baled out and the pilot made a forced landing with the rest of the crew being unwounded.
The centre of aircraft was burnt out but the remainder showed a large number of .303 strikes evenly distributed.
Markings: H in yellow, yellow rings on spinners. No. 8104 on fin.
Engines Jumo 211.
Armament: four 250 kg bombs carried.
ID: 60554, AW: pale green, Lechfeld, 20/1/40 & green, Fl.H.Kdtr. E41/I, 16/8/40 & 21/8/40, FP: L 03989.
Ff: Ltn Johann Kernbach.
Bo: Ofw Willi Schumacher.
Bf: Gefr Robert Riedl.
Bm: Uffz Heinz Agel EKII & Sudeten Medal.

The unit was assumed from the aircraft code and Feldpostnummer.

MAP ID 15 (page 343) **6 September 1940** **Ju88A** **Wn.3176** **F1+LP** **6/KG76**

At sea - off Littlehampton, Sussex. 09.20 hrs.

Aircraft was damaged by AA fire during a raid on Kenley aerodrome and also attacked by fighters before crashing into the sea.
Obltn R Wagner +. NKG.
Uffz F Geyer +. NKG.
Bf: Ogefr Hans Kohn +. Buried at sea. Picked up off Folkestone on 7th September 1940.
Bs: Uffz Heinz Hoenel +. NKG.

| 6 September 1940 | Bf109E-7 | Wn.3736 | O + | 4/LG2 | MAP ID 16 (page 343) |

At sea - The Nore, Sheerness, Kent. 18.15 hrs.

Started from near Calais, at 18.00 hrs on escort duties. Shot down by AA fire at a height of 18,000 ft, the pilot baled out and the aircraft sank.
Markings: O in black.
ID: 53621, AW: grey, O.U., 3/9/40, FP: L 36352.
Ff: Ltn Herbert Gültgen

The pilot during interrogation gave his unit but Air Intelligence had not previously identified the ID disc number or Feldpostnummer of II/LG2.

| 6 September 1940 | Bf109E-7 | Wn.5567 | + C | 6/LG2 | MAP ID 17 (page 343) |

Hawkinge aerodrome, Kent. 18.14 hrs.

Started at 17.30 hrs from a small aerodrome approximately forty miles south-east of Boulogne to escort bombers. The aircraft flew from Cap Gris Nez to the Thames Estuary at a height of 12,000 ft and was hit by AA fire near Chatham, Kent. The petrol tank was hit, the pilot turned for home but ran out of petrol and landed at Hawkinge aerodrome, the pilot running to take cover in a hangar due to being shot at and subsequently wounded. Engine cooling system showed a number of .303 strikes.
Markings: + C in yellow bordered in black, black triangle outlined in white. White rudder, wing tips, the white having been painted on yellow. Spinner blue, white with black vertical stripes. Plate showed BF 109E-4/B, constructed by Wiener Neustadter P.W. werke nr. 5567 dated 1940. Camouflage; two shades of grey on upper surfaces, standard duck egg blue lower surfaces.
Fitted with DB 601/A.1 engine. Mercedes Benz werke nr. 65120.
Armament: two MG17 over engine, two 20 mm cannon in wings. External faired-in bomb rack which appeared to be for carrying 50 kg bombs. In the cockpit there was a selector panel and also a bomb jettisoning handle. A button on the joy stick probably being a bomb release button.
ID: 53623, AW: grey, Braunschweig-Waggum, 13/1/40, FP: -.
Ff: Fw Werner Gottschalk EKI wounded.

The pilot joined his present unit in early August 1940, which he claimed was 6/JG1. He had only made four War Flights to England, all of which had been during the previous few days, including flights to Maidstone and Eastchurch. He had previously been in 4/StG 97 [sic] flying Junkers Ju87s in the Polish and French Campaigns.

This aircraft was taken to the RAE Farnborough for further examination before being used as a display aircraft for fund raising.

Yellow C photographed at Farnborough where it was being evaluated as one of the first Bf109s to be captured fitted with a bomb rack.
Again, white tactical markings are in evidence, this time painted over yellow tactical markings. This may back up a theory that there was a specific order to apply white tactical markings around this time. If so, it was very shortlived as yellow reappeared very soon afterwards and remained for the rest of the Battle.

Below: The 'puss in boots' emblem of 6/LG2.

| 6 September 1940 | Bf110C-4 | Wn.2145 | 3U+ CA | Stab ZG26 | MAP ID 18 (page 343) |

At sea - off Dover, Kent. 09.20 hrs.

Started at 08.50 hrs on escort duties. They had just reached the coast without opposition, when an electric fault developed, one engine caught fire and the pilot baled out. The body of the wireless operator was recovered from the sea on 30th October 1940.
ID: -, AW: grey, Verl, 29/1/40, FP: L 16586.
Ff: Olt Friedrich Viertel injured.
Bf: Uffz Rudolf Roth +. CC 1/209.

The pilot was the Technical Officer of the Geschwader and regularly flew different aircraft.

| 6 September 1940 | Bf110C-4 | Wn.2146 | U8+CL | 3/ZG26 | MAP ID 19 (page 343) |

Cannons Hill Golf Course, Coulsdon, Surrey. 09.33 hrs.

Started from Abbeville. The aircraft was attacked by Hurricanes, the wireless operator being wounded in the hand and the pilot broke off the flight. Shortly afterwards there was an explosion which may have been caused by AA fire, the aircraft going into a spin and the wireless operator baled out from 800 ft The pilot was killed in the aircraft
ID: 60035, AW: grey, Crailsheim, 15/1/40, FP: L 33440.
Ff: Uffz Christoph Kiehn +. CC 5/65.
Bf: Uffz Egon Neuss slightly wounded.

The wireless operator would give no indication of his unit or aircraft lettering. The Feldpostnummer was unknown and the ID disc number was previously encountered with the crews of 3M+AA, U8+BB and 3U+EP, however an undated Staffel list headed '3 Staffel/ I/ZG26' contained the names of both the crew.

Below: Not much remained of U8+CL or its pilot after it plunged into Cannons Hill Golf Course. The carefully placed blanket in the hole tells its own story.

Right: U8+CL photographed shortly before it was shot down over Coulsdon.

MAP ID 20 (page 343)

6 September 1940	Bf110D-0	Wn.3405	3U+HR	7/ZG26

At sea - four miles off Bexhill, Sussex. 09.40 hrs.

Failed to return from operations over England following action by fighters.
AW: white, Garz, 22/2/40, FP: -.
Ff: Fw Leonhard Kaufmann +. NKG.
Bf: Fw Gerhard Schumann 60041/18 +. Folkestone, Kent. Washed up Sandgate, Kent on 6th October 1940.

The ID disc was identified by Air Intelligence to be from 7/ZG76 but the Ausweis is identified with a specialist school at Garz for Zerstörer wireless operators.

ZERSTÖRER GESCHWADER 26 (HORST WESSEL).

There was a certain amount of confusion as to the official unit codes of ZG26 due to the only known aircraft of I Gruppe to have been brought down with legible lettering, (on 18th May 1940), having the code U8+BB. The U8 could not be reconciled with 3U+ - - which was known to be that of ZG26. Papers found on prisoners made repeated references to U8+, where disc numbers and documentary evidence indicated I Gruppe. It was subsequently proven that I Gruppe had the code U8+, while II and III Gruppen had 3U+. In spite of the difference in the first two letters, the third and fourth letters conformed to the usual rules.

The Feldpostnummer's for the Gruppen were:

I Gruppe   L 16586.

II Gruppe   L 35265.

III Gruppe   L 33708.

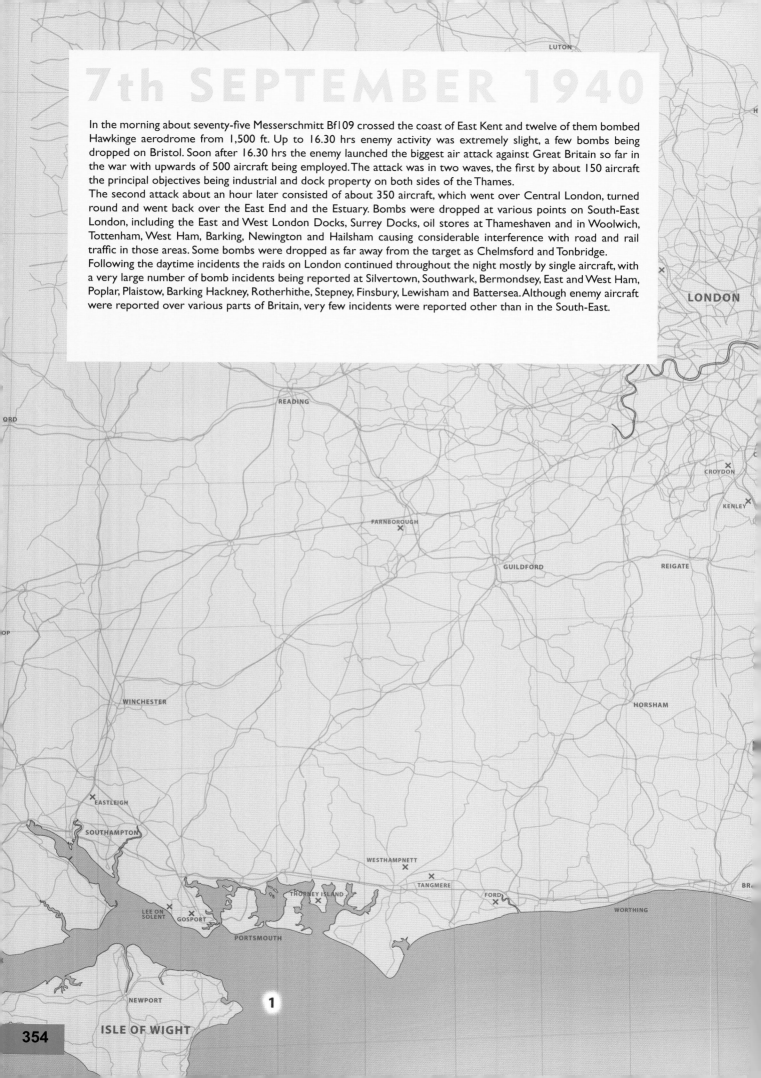

7th SEPTEMBER 1940

In the morning about seventy-five Messerschmitt Bf109 crossed the coast of East Kent and twelve of them bombed Hawkinge aerodrome from 1,500 ft. Up to 16.30 hrs enemy activity was extremely slight, a few bombs being dropped on Bristol. Soon after 16.30 hrs the enemy launched the biggest air attack against Great Britain so far in the war with upwards of 500 aircraft being employed. The attack was in two waves, the first by about 150 aircraft the principal objectives being industrial and dock property on both sides of the Thames.

The second attack about an hour later consisted of about 350 aircraft, which went over Central London, turned round and went back over the East End and the Estuary. Bombs were dropped at various points on South-East London, including the East and West London Docks, Surrey Docks, oil stores at Thameshaven and in Woolwich, Tottenham, West Ham, Barking, Newington and Hailsham causing considerable interference with road and rail traffic in those areas. Some bombs were dropped as far away from the target as Chelmsford and Tonbridge.

Following the daytime incidents the raids on London continued throughout the night mostly by single aircraft, with a very large number of bomb incidents being reported at Silvertown, Southwark, Bermondsey, East and West Ham, Poplar, Plaistow, Barking Hackney, Rotherhithe, Stepney, Finsbury, Lewisham and Battersea. Although enemy aircraft were reported over various parts of Britain, very few incidents were reported other than in the South-East.

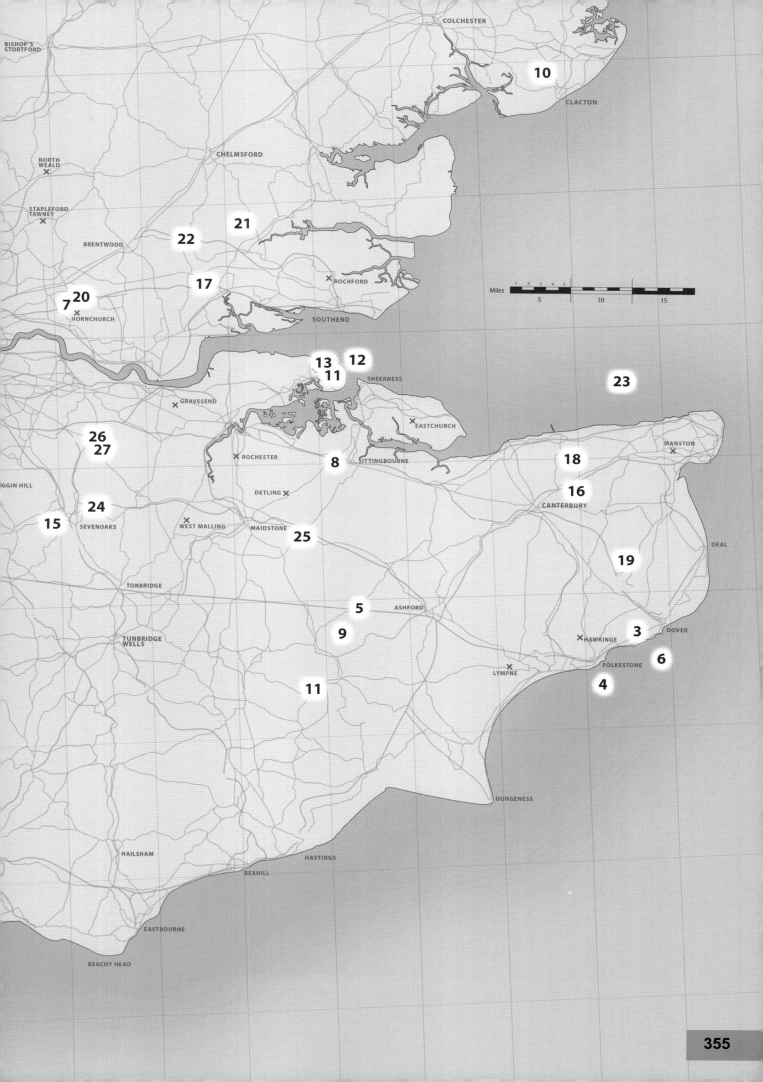

7 September 1940

At sea - off Folkestone, Kent.

Body picked up by a drifter and buried at sea after being searched. Only document an Ausweis previously identified with KG76.
Ogefr Hans Kohn +. Buried at sea.

| 7 September 1940 | Bf110C-5 | Wn.2208 | 5F+MM | | 4(F)/14 | **MAP ID 1** (page 354) |

At sea - ten miles south of Bembridge, Isle of Wight. 09.55 hrs.

Following combat this aircraft exploded in the air and the remains fell into the sea.
Ff: Ltn Hans Gödsche +. CC4/82. Washed ashore Shoreham, Sussex on 22nd November 1940.
Bf: Obltn Gerhard Russel +. NKG.

Left and below: 4U+BL lies forlorn on a Welsh mountainside after hitting the high ground in bad weather.

| 7 September 1940 | Ju88A | | 4U+BL | | 3(F)/123 | **MAP ID 2** (page 354) |

Hafotty - y - Bulch, Mallwyd, Machynlleth, Montgomeryshire, Wales. 12.30 hrs.

Started from Paris-Buc at 09.30 hrs on a photo reconnaissance mission to photograph Liverpool harbour. The crew flew a course Paris – Isle of Wight – Bristol – Liverpool but they were chased from their objective by Spitfires and one engine was hit. Owing to low clouds they crashed into a mountainside.
Markings: B in yellow. Badge: an eagle.
Engines: Jumo 211. Starboard nr. 37956, port nr. 27945.
Armament: two MG15 with ring and bead sight fixed in ball mounting in the cabin Plexiglas firing to the rear. One MG15 forward position standard, one lower rear and one lower forward MG15.

ID: 69006, AW: light brown, Langendiebach, 1/2/40, FP: L 00544.
Ff: Ltn Erich Böhle, L.K.S.F.BRUCK/87 wounded.
Bo: Obltn Hans Kauter 69006/6 wounded.
Bf: Uffz Gotthard Leisler 69006/39 wounded.
Bs: Fw Walter Kobold wounded.

The crew had been carrying out photo-reconnaissance over Liverpool, daily, for some time.
Oberleutnant Friedrichs was Staffelkapitän.

MAP ID 3 (page 354)　　**7 September 1940**　　**Bf109E-4**　　**Wn.3909**　　**8 +**　　**1/JG2**

St. Radigund's Abbey, West Hoogham, Kent. 18.30 hrs.

Took off from Dunkirk on escort duty. While over London at 19,500 ft the aircraft developed engine trouble and the pilot made a good forced landing.
Markings: 8 in white. Yellow rudder and spinner. Badge; a red 'Bonzo', with white tongue and feet.
Engine: DB601 A/1, nr. 21125.
ID: 53522, AW: grey, Würzburg, 20/8/40, FP: L 06779.
Ff: Obltn Adolf Götz EKII.
During interrogation the pilot claimed that he had been with his unit for two weeks.

MAP ID 4 (page 354)　　**7 September 1940**　　**Bf109E-1**　　**Wn.3220**　　**6 + -**　　**5/JG2**

At sea - six miles off Folkestone, Kent. 18.00 hrs.

Started from near St. Omer at 14.30 hrs on bomber escort duty. Intercepted by Spitfires at 13,500 ft on the return journey, the engine being hit.
ID: 57003, AW: white, FP: L 30628.
Ff: Uffz Willi Melchert.
The unit was assumed from the ID disc and Feldpostnummer. The pilot had been posted to his unit two days previously from a fighter school.

MAP ID 5 (page 354)　　**7 September 1940**　　**Bf109E-4**　　**Wn.5385**　　**12 + -**　　**4/JG26**

Sheerlands Farm, Pluckley, three miles south-west of Charing, Kent. 18.00 hrs.

Started at 17.30 hrs to meet and escort bombers returning from London. Hit in fighter action at 21,000 ft which damaged the oil cooler and fuel tank and the pilot force landed the aircraft.
Markings: yellow cowling, and rudder. Spinner white. Shield with Gothic black S and above a Jaguar or Tiger. Previous markings had been KB+JC, painted out. 100 octane mark in a yellow triangle. Camouflage; grey speckled on top.
There was definite evidence of this aircraft had been carrying a bomb. Fuselage was marked with a half inch wide red stripe to give glide bombing angle and had a red bomb jettison handle marked 'Bombennotzug' on the starboard side of the cockpit. The guns on this aircraft had tissue paper placed over the muzzle ends.
ID: 60019, AW: -, FP: L 35136 Brussels.
Ff: Ltn Hans Krug. Staffelkapitän.
Air Intelligence recorded the markings on the aircraft as -+12. This pilot, aged 40, was in the GAF reserve and had done a great deal of civilian flying, taught at a flying school in Spain, prior to the war, returning to Germany on the outbreak of war.

MAP ID 6 (page 354)　　**7 September 1940**　　**Bf109E-4**　　**Wn.735**　　**+ -**　　**6/JG26**

At sea - between Dover and Folkestone. 19.00 hrs.

While returning from escorting bombers to London at a height of 18,000 ft this aircraft was attacked by fighters which damaged both radiators and the pilot eventually baled out over the sea.
Markings: - in brown. Spinner and engine cowling yellow. Badge; a goat.
ID: 60018, AW: white, Dortmund, 5/4/40, FP: L 38561.
Ff: Uffz Ernst Braun.

The pilot stated during interrogation that he had been flying over England, mostly on free-lance patrols for the previous eight weeks. He also named four pilots from his Staffel who had been recently posted missing but their names were not known to Air Intelligence so presumably they were lost over the Channel.

7 September 1940   **Bf109E-4**   **Wn.5390**   **1/JG27**   **MAP ID 7** (page 354)

Rainham Road, Hornchurch, Essex. 17.10 hrs.

On escort duties, at 15,000 ft when collided with a Spitfire, the pilot of which baled out prior to this pilot baling out.
ID: 60327, AW: white, Düsseldorf, FP: -.
Ff: Ltn Günther Genske.

The unit was assumed from the ID disc.

7 September 1940   **Bf109E-1**   **Wn.4840**   **9 +**   **3/JG51**   **MAP ID 8** (page 354)

Oad Street, near Sittingbourne, Kent. 17.45 hrs.

Started from St Inglevert at 17.05 hrs on escort duties. Six aircraft from each of the 1st, 2nd and 3rd Staffeln started together and met a formation of about twenty bombers in mid Channel. This aircraft was hit by AA fire before reaching its objective, the pilot parachuted, the aircraft being completely destroyed and buried in a crater.
Markings: 9 in brown. A plate pertained to show that the aircraft was constructed by Arado nr. 1298, 1940. The pilot also stated that the Staffel colours were 1st Staffel, white; 2nd Staffel, Red and 3rd Staffel, Brown.
ID: 65153, AW: white, 5/8/40, FP: L 13820.
Ff: Gefr Heinrich Werner, Sudeten Medal, wounded.

The pilot claimed that I/JG51 had been based at St.Inglevert since 12th July 1940.

7 September 1940   **Bf109E-3**   **Wn.5091**   **7 +**   **3/JG51**   **MAP ID 9** (page 354)

Bethersden, Kent. 17.45 hrs.

Started from St. Inglevert at 17.15 hrs with other Messerschmitt Bf109s from I/JG51 escorting some twenty-four Dornier Do17s to an attack on the oil storage tanks on the Thames at Thameshaven. Bombs were dropped on the objective and this aircraft was attacked by Spitfires on the way back at a height of 12,000 ft. The petrol tank was hit and the pilot baled out. Aircraft smashed and burnt out.
Markings: 7 in brown. Badge: a mountain goat.
ID: 65153, AW: grey, Krefeld, 16/4/40, signed Hag, FP: L 13820 Frankfurt.
Ff: Uffz Heinz zur Lage EKI.

In preliminary interrogation, the pilot who had received the Iron Cross 1st Class that same morning, stated that they had recently made daily sorties and occasionally two sorties a day, being given an average of two days rest weekly.

7 September 1940   **Bf109E-4**   **Wn.4097**   **11 + I**   **9/JG51**   **MAP ID 10** (page 354)

Little Clacton, near Clacton-on-Sea, Essex. 16.59 hrs.

Aircraft took off from Calais on escort duties to London. Attacked by Spitfires on the return journey, the radiator being hit and the pilot baled out. Aircraft crashed and was completely wrecked.
Markings: 11 in yellow. Yellow rudder, cowling and wing tips. A plate showed werke nr. 4097.
Engine: DB601 A/1 werke nr. 21285, constructed by Niedersachsischer M.W., Braunschweig-Queres.
ID: -, AW: white paper, FP L 29620 Münster, 23/2/40, FP: L 32176.
Ff: Uffz Kurt Koch.

The pilot refused to give his unit under interrogation and his ID disc and Feldpostnummer although identified previously had not been associated with a unit.

7 September 1940   **Bf109E-4**   **Wn.5811**   **11 +**   **1/JG77**   **MAP ID 11** (page 354)

Rolvenden, near Tenterden, Kent. 17.45 hrs.

Started from Northern France at 17.00 hrs on escort duties. This aircraft was shot down by fighters before reaching its objective. A bomb was later found under the fuselage.
There was a red line on the side of the fuselage, pointing forward from the pilot's seat at an angle of 45°; this probably indicated the bombing angle.
ID: 1/JG77, AW: white, Köln Ostheim, 22/1/40, FP: L 32066 Hamburg.
Ff: Ofw Gotthard Goltzsche.

Right: Another Bf109 that was put on display to the public was Gotthard Goltzsche's White 11, seen here with the Lord Mayor of Oldham, Alderman J. R. Buckley, in the cockpit.

MAP ID 12 (page 354)   **7 September 1940   He111P-4   Wn.3078   5J+JP   6/KG4**

At sea - Thames, near the Isle of Grain, Kent. 22.40 hrs.

Started from an aerodrome near the Dutch-German border at 21.00 hrs. Before reaching the objective an AA shell burst close by, stopping one of the engines so three of the crew baled out.
ID: 55538, AW: green, Battle HQ, 4/4/40, 3/9/40 & 6/9/40, FP: -.
Ff: Uffz Richard Klein.
Bo: Olt Walter Klotz 65109/11 +. CC 1/460.
Bf: Uffz Wilhelm Wolf 55537/73 +. CC 1/266.
Bm: Uffz Andreas Knoll +. NKG.
Bs: Gefr Helmuth Beckmann.

| 7 September 1940 | He111H-2 | Wn.2777 | A1+DN | 5/KG53 | **MAP ID 13** (page 354) |

Old Marsh, Isle of Grain. 17.30 hrs.

Started from Lille at 15.00 hrs to bomb Thameshaven. This aircraft bombed the objective and was shot down by a Spitfire from a height of 18,000 ft on the return. The wireless operator was killed and when the crew force landed they set fire to the aircraft.

Markings: D in black, outlined in white. Spinners red.

Engines: Jumo 211 A, one numbered 45388, constructed Dessau.

Armament: five MG15.

ID: 53578 7 65116, AW: white, Fliegerhorstkommandantur E 5/3, 5/9/40 & grey, Ingolstadt, 1/5/40, FP: L 06460.

Ff: Ofw Alfred Pitzka.

Bo: Obltn Heinz Bräuer.

Bf: Ogefr Peter Neumann +. CC 1/61.

Bm: Gefr Ernst Urich wounded.

Bs: Uffz Friedrich Bergmann wounded.

One of the crew gave the unit as 5/KG53, while the ID discs were for KG53 and the Feldpostnummer was for Gruppe II.

The observer,who had nine years service, had kept a complete journal of his career, the highlights were;

29/9/31	15/I.R.11, Dobeln.
1/9/33	Promoted to Oberschutze.
1/8/34	Promoted to Unteroffizier.
16/10/35	7/I.R.103, Erfurt.
1/6/36	Promoted to Feldwebel.
6/10/36	7/I.R.71.
1/10/37	Fliegerhorst Kompanie, Eschwege.
1/2/38	Fliegerhorst Kompanie, Giessen.
1/3/38	Promoted to acting Hauptfeldwebel.
1/12/38	2 Schulerkompanie, Lechfeld. Promoted to Oberfeldwebel.
14/2/40	Luftkriegs Schule 4, Neuhausen.
30/4/40	3 Schulerkompanie, Warsaw.
5/7/40	Erganzungs Kampfgruppe 2, Quedlingburg.
5/8/40	KG53, Giebelstadt.
8/8/40	Hoheres Flieger Ausbildungs Kommando 13. Abteilung IIa. Promoted to Oberleutnant.
4/9/40	5/KG53, Lille.
7/9/40	Shot down.

| 7 September 1940 | Ju88A-1 | Wn.6032 | B3+AM | 4/KG54 | **MAP ID 14** (page 354) |

At sea - North Sea.

Crashed due to unknown causes during operations to London.

ID: 60028, AW: -, FP: 04785 Münster.

Ofw Heinrich Schmitz EKII 60028/7 +. CC 1/215. Washed ashore Southwold, Suffolk 25th October 1940.

Ofw Hans Bremer +. NKG.

Fw Erwin Kalucza +. NKG.

Fw H Lieberknecht +. NKG.

The names of crews of all aircraft of KG54 already reported were known to Air Intelligence and as Oberfeldwebel Schmitz was not among them it was considered that this indicated a further loss. The unit was assumed from ID disc and Feldpostnummer.

Opposite page: A selection of photos showing Uffz Werner Götting who baled out of his Bf109 over Wickhambreaux. The 'White 11' in the bottom photo is believed to be the one he baled out of on 7th September.

| 7 September 1940 | Do17Z | Wn.2596 | F1+BA | Stab KG76 | **MAP ID 15** (page 354) |

Sundridge, one mile west of Sevenoaks, Kent. 18.00 hrs.

On a reconnaissance mission to photograph the bomb damage caused to London Docks. While on its return journey the aircraft was attacked at 16,000 ft by fighters, which killed the pilot and the aircraft went into a dive. The wireless operator baled out and the aircraft crashed into a stream being completely wrecked.

Plate showed aircraft was constructed by Dornier Werke Friedrichshafen R.835.

Armament: two MG15 found.
ID: Bla 71032, AW: yellow, Langendiebach, 1/2/40, FP: -.
Ff: Lt Gottfried Schneider 71032/36 +. CC 9/21.
Bo: Ofw Karl Schneider 71032/36 +. CC 9/21.
Bf: Fw Erich Rosche wounded.
Bm: Uffz Walter Rupprecht +. CC 9/21.

The unit was assumed from the aircraft code given by the crew and the ID disc.
This aircraft was subsequently found to have collided with the Spitfire of F/Lt Pat Hughes of 234 Squadron.

7 September 1940	Bf109E-7	Wn.5798	11 +	1/LG2

Wickhambreaux, five miles east of Canterbury, Kent. 17.35 hrs.

The aircraft was attacked by Spitfires and the pilot baled out, the aircraft being smashed to pieces and was buried in a crater.
Markings: 11 in white. A plate found indicated that aircraft was constructed by B.F.W. Regensburg.
The pilot refused to talk in a preliminary interrogation.
ID: 53532, AW: blue, Jerver, 5/9/40, signed Vogee, FP: -.
Ff: Uffz Werner Götting EKII.

The pilot refused to talk during interrogation so the unit was assumed from the ID disc which was one number below 2/LG2.

MAP ID 16 (page 354)

| 7 September 1940 | Bf110C-4 | Wn.3246 | 3M+BB | Stab I/ZG2 | MAP ID 17 (page 354) |

Kennel Lane, Laindon Common, Essex. 17.30 hrs.

Started from Bergues at 15.45 hrs on escort duties to Thameshaven, the course being: Bergues - Calais - Dover. This aircraft was attacked by Spitfires and the crew baled out. Aircraft was completely wrecked. Markings: B in green. Four stripes visible on tail.
ID: 55564, AW: white, Graz, 20/2/40, FP: L 06173.
Ff: Obltn Gerhardt Granz.
Bf: Fw Willi Schutel.
The unit was assumed from the Feldpostnummer. The Staffelkapitän was Hauptmann Heinlein.

Another day, another smoking hole containing a Bf110. This time it's 3M+BB at Laindon Common with the recovery crew seemingly more interested in the illicit apple picking going on in the foreground!

| 7 September 1940 | Bf110C-4 | Wn.2216 | 3M+LM | 3/ZG2 |

Old Tree Farm, Hoath, near Herne Bay, Kent. 17.20 hrs.

MAP ID 18 (page 354)

Started from near Amiens at 16.00 hrs on escort duties. The whole Staffel, together with Messerschmitt Bf109 units were escorting bombers when this aircraft was attacked by a Spitfire from the rear and an engine hit. The wireless operator parachuted but the pilot remained in the aircraft which crashed and completely burnt out.
Armament: four damaged MGs and two 20 mm cannon found. No armour plate.
ID: 55566, AW: white, Graz, 20/2/40, FP: L 06173.
Ff: Ltn Friedrich Kislinger +. CC 1/417.
Bf: Ogefr Reinhold Dahmke.

The ID disc and Feldpostnummer indicated that the unit was 3/ZG2 while the aircraft markings, 3M+LM*, given by the wireless operator indicated the 4th Staffel. A piece of paper found in the aircraft, dated 5th September 1940 referred to a flight by the pilot in 3M+AM.
*The wireless operator may have deliberately reversed the last two digits to confuse, as 3M+ML would be more consistent with a 3. Staffel machine. Another source quotes 3M+LL for this aircraft.

| 7 September 1940 | Bf110C-4 | Wn.3117 | 3M+FL | 3/ZG2 | MAP ID 19 (page 354) |

Eyethorne, Kent. 17.20 hrs.

Crashed due to fighter action, the crew baled out with wreckage being strewn over several acres after the aircraft blew up in the air.
Markings: F in yellow.
ID: 3 St. ZG 2 & 55566, AW: white, Köln, 13/1/40, FP: L 06173.
Ff: Haupfw Friedrich-Jacob Oligschläger, 7/35T.ZG.2 +. CC 1/324.
Bf: Ofw Ernst Otterbach 35566/9 +. CC 1/325.

Details of the unit were found on documents and confirmed by the ID disc. Air Intelligence recorded the name of the pilot as Feldwebel Friedrich Jakob.

Soldiers pick through fragments of the Bf110 3M+FL at Eyethorne north of Dover. Pieces include a parachute, compressed air bottle and a flare pistol.

MAP ID 20 (page 354)

7 September 1940	Bf110D-0	Wn.3334	A2+NH	Stab II/ZG2

Park Corner Farm, Hacton Lane, Hornchurch, Essex. 17.10 hrs.

Following fighter action, aircraft exploded in mid air and wreckage scattered over a wide area, with the crew being blown out they were unable to deploy their parachutes.
Markings: white N on one wing.
Ff: Ltn Kurt Schünemann 53585/4 +. CC 1/366.
Bf: Uffz Hans Mescheder 53585/50 +. CC 1/367.

The pilot was the Technical Officer of his Gruppe.

MAP ID 21 (page 354)

7 September 1940	Bf110D-0	Wn.3185	A2+BH	4/ZG2

Ramsden Bellhouse, near, Wickford, Essex. 17.15 hrs.

Aircraft crashed and wrecked following fighter action.
Markings: B on end of wingtips and spinners white. 3185 on rear end of fuselage.
No armament or armour found.
ID: 69022, AW: white, Düsseldorf, 8/2/40, signed Major Heimberg, FP: L 03675.
Ff: Ltn Hans Dietrich Abert 53585/M +. CC 1/372.
Bo: Uffz Karl Scharf 69022/19 +. CC 1/458.

The unit was assumed from the aircraft lettering A2+B -, with the white B indicating the 1st or 4th Staffel.

MAP ID 22 (page 354)

7 September 1940	Bf110D-0	Wn.3328	A2+JH	4/ZG2

Bullers Farm, Little Burstead, Essex. 17.30 hrs.

Following fighter action port engine was set on fire and was burning as the aircraft crashed. The pilot was wounded and baled out. Aircraft wrecked and mostly burnt out.
No armament or armour plate found.
Markings: J in white and two stripes on the tail. Badge; a dragon.
ID: 53585, AW: -, FP: L 06173.
Ff: Ltn Karl Stix wounded.
Bf: Gefr Heinrich Hetz +. CC 1/459.

Air Intelligence assumed the unit from the aircraft lettering and the Feldpostnummer to be 1/ZG2.

At sea - five miles off Birchington, Kent. 17.20 hrs.

Started at 15.00 hrs on escort duties to the Thames Estuary. On the return journey this aircraft was attacked by Spitfires and force landed on the sea.
Markings: M in yellow.
ID: 69024, AW: white, Düsseldorf, 8/6/40, FP: -.
Ff: Obltn Willi Brede EKI.
Bf: Uffz August Galla +. CC 1/435.

The pilot under interrogation gave the code details of his aircraft as A2+LM with the L in yellow, so Air Intelligence assumed he was with the 4th Staffel.

Below: As London burned on 7th September John Peskett was still as busy as ever in Essex, investigating the last three Bf110s on the previous page.

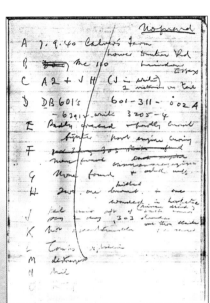

INTELLIGENCE REPORT - ZERSTÖRERGESCHWADER 2.

The markings on aircraft of this unit were:

		Marking.	Disc.	Feldpostnummer.
Gruppe I	Stab I	3M+ - B	55564	L 06173.
	Staffel 1	3M+ - H	55564	'
	Staffel 2	3M+ - K	55565	'
	Staffel 3	3M+ - L	55566	'
Gruppe II	Stab II	A2+ - C	69022	03675.
	Staffel 4	A2+ - H	69022	'
	Staffel 5	A2+ - K	69023	'
	Staffel 6	A2+ - L	69024	'

Major Ott who was lost on 11th August 1940 was the Gruppenkommandeur of I/ZG2, his successor, Hauptmann Kuebel was lost the following day. The third Kommandeur was Hauptmann Heinlein who was previously Staffelkapitän of 6/ZG2. Between 23rd August 1940 and 5th September 1940 aircraft of Gruppe I were to be fitted with DB601N engines, as was II/ZG26 and 3/ZG26, armour plate was also to be fitted.

The following losses were unaccounted for:

Code.	Date.	Werke nr.	
3M+AH	11/8/40	2127.	
3M+ - -	11/8/40	3078	Major Ott.
3M+LL	11/8/40	3123	
3M+ - -	12/8/40	3115	
3M+ - -	12/8/40	3316	Major Kuelbel.
3M+HK	12/8/40	3515.	

Aircraft with Gruppe I of ZG 2 on 12th August 1940..

Stab I		1st Staffel		2nd Staffel		3rd Staffel	
3120	3M+CB	2127	3M+AH	2070	3M+BK	3561	3M+AL
3246	3M+BB	2142	3M+BH	3075	3M+CK	3183	3M+BL
3621	3M+DB	2123	3M+CH	3319	3M+DK	2820	3M+CL
		3087	3M+DH	2065	3M+EK	3083	3M+DL
		2140	3M+EH	3085	3M+FK	3113	3M+EL
		2055	3M+FH	2134	3M+GK	3117	3M+FL
		2057	3M+GH	3515	3M+HK	2132	3M+GL
		3198	3M+HH	3606	3M+HK*	2133	3M+HL
		3208	3M+KH	3622	3M+HK*	3122	3M+KL
		3201	3M+LH	3118	3M+KK	3123	3M+LL
		3623	3M+LH*	3120	3M+LK	2216	3M+LL*
		3616	3M+MH	2131	3M+LK*	3079	3M+ML
		3316	3M+MK	3317	3M+NL		
		3606	3M+MK*	2220	3M+NL*		
		3193	3M+NK				

* - replacement aircraft

Aircraft with 4/ZG2, stationed at Guyancourt on 2nd August 1940.

A2+AH	3186	Crashed.
A2+BH	3185	ok.
A2+CH	3197	ok.
A2+DH	3181	ok.
A2+EH	3065	ok.
A2+FH	3554	ok.
A2+GH	3191	Missing.
A2+HH	3173	ok.
A2+IH	3187	ok.
A2+JH	3328	ok.
A2+KH	3199	Crashed.
A2+LH	3188	Port engine giving trouble.
A2+MH	3576	ok.
A2+NH	3324	ok.

With more cloudy conditions than the previous day very little enemy air activity was reported during the day and confined to a raid on Dover at 12.00 hrs which was bombed from 15,000 ft and at 12.40 hrs. Detling and West Malling were targeted. The attack came into Chatham and there split, part going towards Biggin Hill and part to North Weald, being reported as fifty Dornier Do17s, led by three Junkers Ju88s at 16,000 ft with an escort in three parts; Messerschmitt Bf110s at the same level, fifty Messerschmitt Bf109s five miles behind at 25,000 ft and twenty Messerschmitt Bf109s 4,000 ft below the bombers. This raid was intercepted and the leading Junkers Ju88s and Dornier Do17s were attacked with the result that the formation broke up and turned east. It is probable that they did not reach their objective as most bombs were scattered across Kent. Raids on London were renewed just before dusk at 19.45 hrs when forty bombers came in over Beachy Head and continued throughout the night with considerable damage being caused to rail and road communications, with many serious fires being started. The heaviest bombing occurred in the riverside districts but minor and seemingly indiscriminate bombing was widespread.

| 8 September 1940 | Bf109E-4 | Wn.867 | | 3/JG53 | MAP ID 24 (page 354) |

Seal, near Sevenoaks, Kent. 12.40 hrs.

Shot down during combat with fighters and dived into the ground with the engine at full power, the pilot inside.
ID: -, AW: grey, E.5/VIII, 13/8/40, FP: 36621.
Ff: Uffz Bernhardt Adelwart +. CC 1/164.

There was nothing to indicate the unit apart from the Ausweis which had previously been encountered with 2/JG3.

| 8 September 1940 | Do17Z | Wn.3415 | U5+LN | 5/KG2 | MAP ID 25 (page 354) |

Leeds near Maidstone, Kent. 12.40 hrs.

While flying in a formation of three aircraft, hit by AA fire in the bomb compartment and exploded, destroying the other two Dorniers flying in the neighbourhood. Wreckage was distributed over several miles, the major portions falling on a camp occupied by the 21st Battalion New Zealand Expeditionary Force. When the souvenir hunters had finished, there was nothing much remaining.
Aircraft manufactured under licence by Henschel.
ID: 53577, AW: grey, Fl.H.Kdtr.44/XI,1/9/40, FP: -.
Ff: Obltn Martin Ziems +. Maidstone, Kent.
Bo: Uffz Heino Flick +. NKG. Buried as an unknown German Airman at Maidstone, Kent.
Bs: Uffz Wilhelm Selter +. NKG. Buried as an unknown German Airman at Maidstone, Kent.
Bf: Uffz Wilhelm Trost +. NKG. Buried as an unknown German Airman at Maidstone, Kent.

The ID disc recovered was from a school and had previously been encountered with KGs 1, 2, 3, 40 and 53.

| 8 September 1940 | Do17Z | Wn.1130 | U5+FN | 5/KG2 | MAP ID 26 (page 354) |

Farningham Road Railway Station, Kent. 12.40 hrs.

Exploded in the air due to other exploding Dornier in the vicinity which was hit by AA fire.
ID: 58221, AW: grey, Fürth 1/2/40, FP: -.
Ff: Ltn Otto Landenberger +. CC 9/23.
Bo: Ogefr Friedrich Lotter 53576/268 +. CC 9/23.
Bf: Ofw Max Ströbel injured.
Bm: Gefr Paul Schütze 53576/268 +. CC 9/23.

Right: Ltn Otto Landenberger who died in the explosion of U5+FN.

Near Farningham Road Railway Station, Kent. 12.45 hrs.

Took off 11.12 hrs to attack the Thames docks. Crashed due to exploding Dornier in the vicinity. A local AA battery opened fire; the first round was the sighter and with the second they claimed to have destroyed three aircraft.

This crew made a short formation flight in the morning from 09.19 to 09.49 hrs possibly from Lille.

Markings: B in black, outlined in white.

Armament: ten 50 kg bombs carried.

ID: 58214, AW: grey, Fl.H.Kdtr.44/XI, grey 1/2/40, Fürth, signed Major Wehr, grey 17/5/40 Fl.H.Kdtr.E.29/XII signed Holbech & grey 1/4/40 Ausbach signed Prauchel, FP: -.

Ff: Olt Joachim Schneider wounded.

Bo: Uffz Josef Schuhmacher wounded.

Bf: Ogefr Hans Hoffmann wounded.

Bs: Flgr Willi Kohl wounded.

Below and right: The remarkable downing of three Do17s by one flak burst left wreckage strewn over a wide area. These pieces fell near Farningham railway station around lunchtime on 8 September.

There was very little enemy activity during the day until after 17.00 hrs when a large force of enemy aircraft approached London. They were quickly dispersed, although some bombs were dropped, mostly in the suburbs south of the River Thames. Bombs also fell in Kent, also notably on Canterbury. The scheme of attack was that six formations of twenty to thirty aircraft each crossed the coast at about five minute intervals, between North Foreland and Dungeness and headed for the Thames Estuary. Two of these formations were bombers only, one was bombers with escort and three were fighters only. The latter were probably an offensive patrol covering Kent and the Estuary, and of the former, one formation turned back, bombing Canterbury on the way, while others appeared to fly across the Biggin Hill area where they were intercepted and turned, part going east and part to the south-west. The whole of these operations appeared to be a screen for the main attack which was delivered by a formation of about 150 bombers and fighters crossing the coast at Hastings and aiming for London. They were intercepted and appeared to split, part crossing over South London, where bombs were dropped at random and south of London and out by the Estuary, and part returning between Selsey and Dungeness.

Further interceptions followed and appeared to break the formations up again, one squadron reporting forty Junkers Ju88s, Heinkel He111s and fighters escaping southwards at full speed and lowering height, over Beachy Head. It appeared probable that about 100 to 150 bombers were operating in five complete gruppen, including III/KG1, III/KG53, II/KG30 and III/KG30, the KG30 units having been recently transferred from Norway and Denmark. This, with the fighters, gives a total of 300 to 350 aircraft.

The attacks on London once again were continued at nightfall by relays of single aircraft, with aircraft coming in at dusk from Cherbourg via the Isle of Wight and from Dieppe between Beachy Head and Dungeness; at 02.00 hrs aircraft came in over the Thames Estuary. Apart from attacks on railways, bombing appeared wholly indiscriminate. Two major fires were started in the City and two termini were put out of action (Charring Cross and Fenchurch Street). A serious fire was also started at Woolwich Arsenal.

Elsewhere in the country there was rather more activity than on previous nights. A large number of bombs were dropped on Canterbury with a few bombs also falling in rural areas across England, Wales and Scotland. Dover was also shelled for the two and a half hours leading up to midnight.

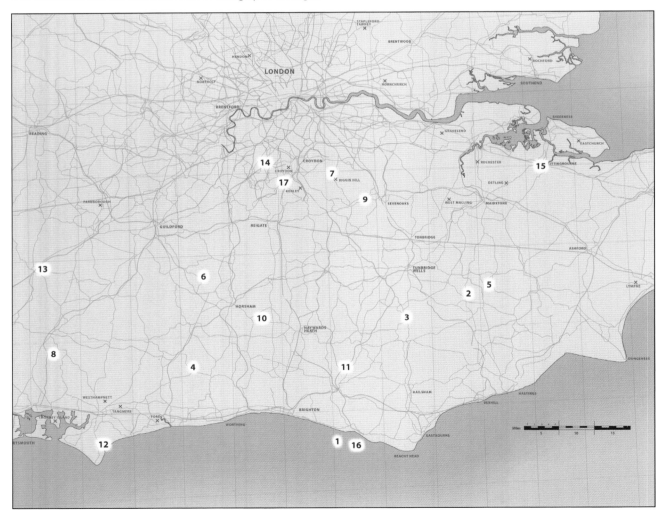

9 September 1940   Body Recovered

At sea - Brancaster, Norfolk.

A body was washed ashore, had been in the sea a considerable time. Four bodies had been washed up at the same place on 20th August 1940 having the same disc number belonging to 4/KG3.
ID: 52591, AW: -, FP: -.
Crew: -.

MAP ID I (page 368)

9 September 1940   Bf109E-1   Wn.6138   4/JG3

At sea - six miles off Newhaven, Sussex. 17.55 hrs.

Started from near Calais at 17.00 hrs escorting bombers to the London Docks. The formation consisted of about forty bombers and an escort of sixty mixed Messerschmitt Bf109s and Messerschmitt Bf110s. As the bombers were heading for London, there was a slight engagement with fighters near Dover at 17.50 hrs and shortly afterwards the engine of this aircraft began to fail and escorted by his pair in the Rotte (Feldwebel Kortlopel), turned for home. At 22,000 ft, suddenly his pair dived sharply under control and for no apparent reason, leaving this pilot to his fate; he tried to reach the French Coast but failed.
ID: -, AW: dark grey, Zerbst, 10/5/40, FP: L 29166.
Ff: Fw August-Wilhelm Müller.

The pilot gave the identity of his unit as Stab II/JG3. The pilot had been in the German Air Force Reserve for five years and was called up at the outbreak of war. He was wounded in the fighting in France, near the Somme, and had made twenty-two flights against England, mostly to South London. Before the war he was an international hockey player and represented Germany against England, in 1934-36 and 1937.

MAP ID 2 (page 368)

9 September 1940   Bf109E-1   Wn.6316   6 + I   7/JG3

Coopers Field, Rosemary Farm, Flimwell, Sussex. 17.35 hrs.

Started at 17.15 hrs on a free-lance patrol consisting of one Staffel, along the English Coast. While flying at 25,000 ft, when over the coast, they were surprised by a Spitfire coming out of the sun and shot this aircraft from behind through the engine. The aircraft landed with its undercarriage retracted and was in good condition.
Markings: 6 and I, white with black edges. Yellow spinner and rudder. Aircraft constructed by Gerhardt Fieseler, Cassel, werke nr. 6316, 1940.
Engine: DB601 A, constructed by N.M.W. Braunschweig series nr. 21178.

Right: Another 109 that ended up at Farnborough because of its bomb carrying capability was 'White 6' that came down at Coopers Field. It is seen here with the cowling of 'Yellow C' in the foreground. (see page 350). The report mentions a yellow spinner but this could have been a misinterpretation of 'yellow nose'. Alternatively a replacement spinner may have been fitted.

Armament: four MG17. Standard bulkhead and armoured shield behind pilot's head. This aircraft was fitted with dive and horizontal bomb gear between pilot's knees apparently for four bombs, size unknown. Red line on glass indicated a dive angle of about 45°. Usual landing flaps used to limit speed in dive bombing, having lines to show 0°, 10°, 20°, 30°, 40°; the 40° line being marked in red. Fuel 87 octane.

ID: 57217, AW: white, Dortmund, 11/5/40, signed Krug, FP: 13116.

Ff: Uffz Matthias Massmann.

The pilot was a reservist who had done a little flying each year and was called up on 3rd September 1939, joining his operational unit at the beginning of the French Campaign.

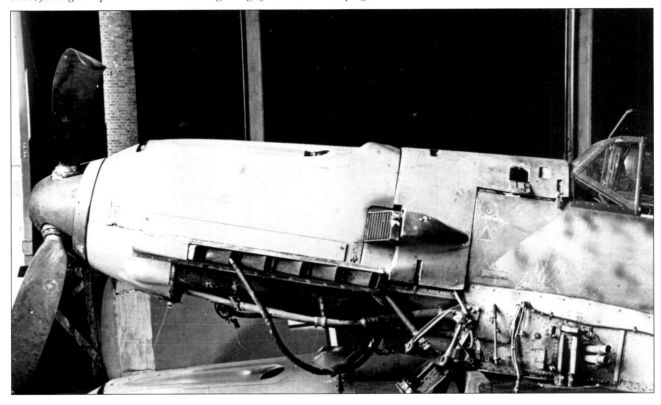

| 9 September 1940 | Bf109E-4 | Wn.1394 | < + | Stab I/JG27 |

MAP ID 3 (page 368)

Knowle Farm, Mayfield, Sussex. 17.45 hrs.

While flying at about 16,000 ft two Spitfires suddenly appeared above and this aircraft was shot through the radiator with the first burst. Turning for home the engine began to overheat and the aircraft landed in good condition, except for a damaged undercarriage. At the time of combat the formation was fairly near to London but the pilot could not see it because of a slight mist.

Markings: yellow nose and rudder. Upper surfaces of the fuselage and wings were painted a dark grey-green, the side of the fuselage and undersurfaces light blue. Crest on nose, a yellow jaguar's head with smiling negress wearing a white ear ring. Shield; map of Africa with tiger's head. Aircraft constructed by Erla MW Leipzig, werke nr. 1394 dated 22nd November 1939. Wings manufactured by Junkers, Dessau.

Engine: DB601 A. A coloured plate on front of engine bore letters H.M.F. in the middle of a six pointed star. Engine plate showed Mercedez Benz, Daimler Benz AG, werke nr. 90. Berlin/Marianfelde, series no. 11366. Fuel 88 octane.

ID: 60324, AW: white paper, Düsseldorf 14/1/40, FP: -.

Ff: Obltn Günther Bode. Gruppe Adjutant.

Above: Obltn Günther Bode

The shield on the aircraft had previously been identified with JG27.

The aircraft was initially covered in camouflage netting by the military prior to removal to Stanhay's Garage, Ashford for exhibition and later at Barretts Garage, Canterbury.

AN EYEWITNESS: MRS SHELMERDINE, KNOWLE FARM.

After the aircraft had crash landed the pilot climbed out and pulled off his flying helmet. All the men on the farm rushed up to him with pitchforks, but my husband arrived on the scene and sorted things out. My husband was a tall military looking figure and the German pilot said to him 'Ah ... Officer?' I could tell that he was also a gentleman by his perfect manner and his bearing. He started to play with my black Labrador, but I called him away. The German airman seemed upset, and said 'oh, but he lufs me, Ja?' To which I replied, 'Yes, but we don't.' He was taken down to Mark Cross Police Station and upon arrival there he asked if he could use the toilet. This he was allowed to do and he promptly disposed of all his personal papers. The plane itself was in the big 'twelve acre' field, the military fenced it off and covered it with camouflage netting but it stopped there for at least three weeks. This worried me because it was near the house and buildings and I was sure it would be seen from the air.

Above and below: Obltn Günther Bode's Bf109 before and after being shot down near London on 9th September. The I/JG27 emblem can be seen under the camouflage netting (left).

More views of Obltn Günther Bode's Bf109 on display in Ashford. Note that the yellow cowling was not painted over the uppersurface camouflage.

Charity Farm, Cootham, near Storrington, Sussex. 17.50 hrs.

Started from Calais, escorting bombers to London. Following an attack by a fighter at 20,000 ft from below and astern, the radiator and petrol tank were hit, and the pilot force landed, the aircraft being in good condition.

Markings: 13+ -, long red dash with white edging, 13 in black with white border. Cowling and rudder yellow. Aircraft constructed by Henschel FW.

Engine: DB601 constructed by Henschel nr. 30155.

Armament: Standard. No bombs found but bomb release gear for four 30 kg [sic] bombs fitted to the bottom of the cockpit panel with release button on control column. Four eyes fitted below the fuselage for bomb rack.

ID: 53537, AW: -, FP: -.

Ff: Obltn Erwin Daig.

Below: Erwin Daig's Black 13 photographed on display to the public, possibly in Dudley, West Midlands.

MAP ID 5 (page 368) **9 September 1940** **Bf109E-1** **Wn.6280** **7 + -** **6/JG27**

Mounts Farm, Benenden, Kent. 18.15 hrs.

Started at 17.30 hrs escorting about forty bombers attacking London. Flying at between 19,000 and 21,000 ft the pilot got careless and dropped too far behind; suddenly he was peppered by a Spitfire, dived down to 10,000 ft and baled out, his aircraft diving into the ground at speed.
Markings: 7 + - in yellow.
ID: 55538, AW: red linen, Fürth, 5/5/40, FP: 37472.
Ff : Uffz Georg Rauwolf EKII.

The pilot had completed eighteen War Flights since moving to his operational unit in June, from an Erganzungs Staffel at Merseburg.

MAP ID 6 (page 368) **9 September 1940** **Bf109E-4** **Wn.1617** **7/JG27**

Roman Gate Cottage, Rudgwick, Sussex. 18.00 hrs.

Took off from the Cherbourg area. Crashed following a dog fight over Horsham Police Station, the wreckage being completely burnt and destroyed. Pilot baled out but was found dead.
Markings: five victory bars painted on the tail.
ID: 65115, AW: white on black backing, Köln, 9/5/40, FP: -.
Ff: Uffz Karl Born EKI, Four Years Service Medal 51515/16 +. CC 1/26.

This airman was awarded his EKI on 5th September 1940. From the pilot's pay book the following information was deduced:
5/9/40   A.B.School, Klagenfurt.
1/2/40   Jagd Fl.Sch., Werneuchen.
12/5/40 3/Erg. Jagd Gruppe.
25/5/40 L 27018 (believed to be Regierungsinspekteur der Luftwaffe.
5/8/40   1 St. III/JG27. Jesau.

Pilot was initially buried at Hill's Cemetery, Horsham, Sussex.

MAP ID 7 (page 368) **9 September 1940** **Bf109E-4** **Wn.1508** **5 +** **1/JG53**

Cherry Tree Farm, Old Jail Inn, near Biggin Hill, Kent. 18.00 hrs.

Started at 17.00 hrs escorting bombers attacking an aerodrome east of London. This aircraft was the left support of a Kette flying in Vic, which was itself the left Vic of a Staffel, at 22,000 ft. On the return flight, the bombers having bombed their objective, the formation was attacked by five Spitfires from the rear, port side. The first burst set fire to this aircraft, and the pilot baled out suffering severe burns. The aircraft crashed and was totally destroyed on crashing.
Markings: 5 in white. Red band round engine cowling, spinner dark green. On the underside of one of the wings, towards the trailing-edge, were two small discs about the size of a penny, painted like an RAF roundel, with the date 13th August 1940; these appeared to be patches covering bullet holes.
Armament: two 20 mm cannon found in the wreckage of wings.
ID: 67005, AW: grey, Darmstadt, FP: -.
Ff: Fw Heinrich Hönisch badly burned.

The pilot would not give away any information about his unit even though in great pain. He said he knew all about British aerodromes as British prisoners in Germany gave away such a lot of information when interrogated.

MAP ID 8 (page 368) **9 September 1940** **Bf109E** **Wn.6139** **1 + I** **8/JG53**

Sunwood Farm, Ditcham, near South Harting, Hampshire. 18.15 hrs.

Following fighter action, aircraft dived into the ground and was buried in a crater, being destroyed by fire.
Armament: two MG17 recovered, along with the standard armoured bulkhead.
ID: Schüler Komp.Sch.Fl.Ausb.Regt.31, AW: -, FP: -.
Ff: Gefr Peter Becker +. CC 6/157.

The pilot's ID disc was the only identification discovered but only indicated that he had recently passed out of a school.

Sundridge, near Sevenoaks, Kent.
18.00 hrs.

At 16.00 hrs this crew picked up their escort over Guines en-route to attack an aerodrome near London, the whole of I/KG 1 taking part. They bombed the target successfully and during the return flight were attacked by Spitfires from the rear which damaged the cooling system and wounded two of the crew. One engine stopped and intercom was shot away. The flight engineer baled out but the rest of the crew remained in the aircraft, the aircraft crashing with its undercarriage retracted and the starboard wing was smashed. The crew tried to set fire to the aircraft with an incendiary bomb but this failed to operate. Both airscrews showed .303 strikes, also on starboard nose, port upper surface of fuselage, twenty in the starboard wing, fifty on the port lower side of the fuselage and six on the port wing and engine.

Armament: six MG15 in standard positions. Lotfe 7B bomb sight. A note gave the bomb load as four 250 kg bombs and two flambe bombs.

Markings: spinners painted dark green. Shield; an eagle biting a lion's neck.

ID 53549, Tr.Gr.z.b.V.9., AW: white, Nordhausen,1/5/40 & 29/2/40, FP: L 02110.

Ff: Obltn Erich Kiunka EKII.
Bo: Uffz Anton Stumbaum.
Bf: Uffz Erich Marks wounded.
Bm: Ofw Alfred Heidrich.
Bs: Gefr Heinrich Reinecke wounded.

A note found in the aircraft had descriptions and drawings of Mildenhall and Sywell aerodromes which may have been the target.

Above: One for the grandchildren! A man poses with the battered starboard engine of He111 V4+BL on display at Sevenoaks.

Church Field, Newells Farm, Nuthurst, Sussex. 18.00 hrs.

Took off 15.30 hrs with four 250 kg bombs; target the London Docks; the same mission having been carried out successfully the previous day. Fifteen aircraft set out all flying in a Ketten Vic astern led by Oberleutnant Metzatin. Although the Geschwaderkommandeur, Oberst Rieckhoff, should have been flying in this aircraft, he was actually with Oberleutnant Gollnesch in 4D+FA. Before reaching the objective the formation was attacked by twelve Spitfires, the Perspex roof, together with the machine guns was jettisoned, the oil radiators were hit and the pilot made a belly landing.

Engines: 211B, manufactured by Junkers AG, Zwigwerk Kothen-Anhalt. Nrs. 53378 on 11th April 1940 and 53078 on 17th February 1940.

Bombsight standard BZG2.

ID: 62757 & 62755, AW: white paper, E.13/IV, 7/9/40, FP: L 30733 & L 26148.

Ff: Obltn Rolf Heim EKII, Four Years Service Medal.
Bo: Uffz Josef Beck EKII, Austrian, Sudeten (Prague Bar), Four Years Service Medals.
Bf: Fw A Fuhs.
Bs: Uffz Walter Baustian.

Aircraft Log Book gave the following details:
Junkers Ju88A-5 Class C.
Werke Nr. & Marks: 274 PM+ZY.
Place of manufacture: Bernburg.
Max. All up weight: 11,775 kgs.
Max. Landing weight: 9,305 kgs.
Max. Speed in horizontal flight: 470 kph.
Max. Speed in dive, without dive brakes: up to 2,000 metres, 675 kph., over 2,000 metres, 600 kph.
Max. Speed in dive, with dive brakes from all heights 550 kph.

After a 34 minute trial flight on 29th May 1940 this aircraft was flown to Dessau and put through various test flights by Aschenbrenner. After 7.54 flying hours, the first B.A.L. (Govt. test) flight took place at Dessau on 16th July 1940. A second B.A.L flight was made on 21st July 1940 after 9.45 hours. The final acceptance was after 15.30 hours. The following day the aircraft was flown from Dessau to Jutterborg-Waldlanger and then to Aalborg the next day where it went into service with KG30.

Below: Showing signs of having been in situ for several days already, Rolf Heim's Ju88 4D+AA starts to look like a piece of modern sculpture.

| 9 September 1940 | Ju88A-2 | Wn.5074 | 4D+KK | Stab II/KG30 | MAP ID I I (page 368) |

Court House Farm, Barcombe, Sussex. 17.40 hrs.

Target London Docks, carrying four 250 kg bombs. Before reaching the objective, this aircraft was intercepted by several Spitfires at 16,000 ft. With both engines hit, the pilot made a forced landing and the aircraft was burnt out. The crew thought that they had scuttled all their bombs but one still remained in the aircraft

Markings: first K in red, outlined in white; second K in black, outlined in white. Spinners red. Figure '93' on top of rudder had been painted out. Shield; red bomb graticule obscuring an umbrella.

Engines: Jumo 211, starboard nr. B45045b.

The Royal Engineers removed armament and 'one 550 lb.' bomb.

ID: 62747 & 62750, AW: Grey, Perleberg, 2/7/40 & 15/8/40, FP: L 26681.

Ff: Ltn Hans-Gert Gollnisch.

Bo: Uffz Willi Rolf.

Bf: Uffz Willi Hamerla.

Bs: Uffz Ernst Deibler 62747/18 +. CC 4/128.

The Staffel number was assumed from the aircraft marking and the ID discs and Feldpostnummer are Gruppe II.

From eye witness accounts the Junkers collided with stakes that had been placed in the field to prevent enemy gliders from landing and was badly damaged. A local farm worker, William Barton, was the first on the scene and when he approached the aircraft he saw three airmen arguing amongst themselves. After setting fire to their aircraft they presented Barton with a pistol and indicated their readiness to surrender. Shortly after this, the body of a fourth airman was found besides the aircraft. He had been shot dead. On Diebler's body was found German, Belgian, Danish and French money.

Right: Ju88 4D+KK burns in a field at Court House Farm near Barcombe. One of the crew members that set fire to the aircraft was Uffz Willi Rolf (inset).

378

Pagham Harbour, Sussex. 17.50 hrs.

Started from Antwerp, with objective Woolwich. Aircraft landed following fighter action, the starboard engine and both radiators being hit. Aircraft half covered at high tide.

Markings: A in blue, with white edges. Crest; diving black eagle on yellow background. Aircraft constructed by Junkers.

Armament standard. Only the back of the pilot's seat armoured with 8 mm plate.

ID: 62756, AW: green 17/7/40 & white 30/1/40, Parchim, FP: L 32091.

Major Johann Hackbarth badly wounded. Gruppenkommandeur.

Ofw Hans Manger badly wounded.

Uffz Willi Sawallisch +. CC 1/98.

Gefr Friederich Petermann 62756/81 +. CC 1/75.

Air Intelligence could derive very little information as few documents were recovered but the airmen had Belgian and Danish money in their pockets. They interpreted that the werke nummer was 3216.

On the tail fin was what appeared to be a Victory bar and the letter A in red, outlined in blue. Willi Sawallisch was originally buried at Chichester Cemetery while Friedrich Petermann was buried at Bognor Regis Cemetery.

Below: The young Gefr Friederich Petermann poses for a studio photo in his new Luftwaffe uniform.

Below right: The last photo taken of Friederich, lying dead in Pagham Harbour. Just one of the hundreds of young lives lost during the Battle of Britain.

Below: Peterman's Junkers Ju 88 came down in the shallows of Pagham Harbour.

More views of 4D+AD in Pagham Harbour. The tidal variation is apparent throught the photos. The diving eagle emblem was common for all aircraft of KG30, with the background colour changing to identify the Gruppe. White = I Gruppe, red = II Gruppe and yellow = III Gruppe.

| 9 September 1940 | He111H-2 | Wn.2630 | A1+ZD | Stab III/KG53 | MAP ID 13 (page 368) |

Southfield Farm, Chawton, near Alton, Hampshire. 17.50 hrs.

At 18,000 ft the aircraft was suddenly attacked by fighter, one wing came off and the aircraft crashed in a spin. Aircraft was completely wrecked on crashing, probably due to bombs on board exploding and wreckage was distributed over a wide area. One crater caused by a bomb explosion was twelve feet in diameter and eight feet deep. Nearby one unexploded 250 kg bomb was found with a delayed action fuse.
ID: 69041, AW: grey, Giebelstadt, 1/2/40, FP: L 03171.
Ff: Oscar Broderix baled out.
Bo: Obltn Kurt Meineke baled out wounded.
Bf: Fw Ernst Wendorff 69041/11 +. CC 5/304.
Bm: Fw Wilhelm Wenninger 69041/8 +. CC 5/306.
Bs: Fw Willi Döring 60553/79 +. CC 5/305.

The unit details were found in documents on the aircraft and the ID disc number had been previously encountered in Stab III/KG53.

| 9 September 1940 | Bf110C-4 | Wn.3298 | L1+DL | 15(Z)/LG1 | MAP ID 14 (page 368) |

Maori Sports Club, Old Malden Lane, Worcester Park, Surrey. 18.00 hrs.

Attacked by two Hurricanes and aircraft exploded after hitting the ground with wreckage being scattered over a large area.
Markings: on two pieces of fuselage part of the yellow letter D outlined in red was found. Evidence of whitewash being used was found on pieces of wing.
ID: -, AW: -, FP: L 14418 Frankfurt.
Ff: Uffz Alois Pfaffelhuber 52603/23 +. CC 1/329.
Bf: Uffz Otto Kramp +. CC 1/328.

The Feldpostnummer was found on two letters, the latest dated 27th August 1940 and had been associated with 15/LG1 but also could be that of a Ergänzungs Staffel.

The pilot's diary was found which started when he transferred an Messerschmitt Bf110 L1+EL of V/LG1 from Mannheim-Sandhofen – Wiesbaden on 16th May 1940. Later entries were:

21/7/40	Me 110	L1+FL	Sandhofen – Le Bourget.
21/7/40	Me 110	L1+FL	Le Bourget – Caen.
23/7/40	Me 110	KF+VA	Illesheim – Le Bourget.
23/7/40	Me 110	KF+VA	Le Bourget – Caen.
29/7/40	Me 110		Illesheim – Le Bourget.
29/7/40	Me 110		Le Bourget – Caen.
18/8/40	Me 110	SD+BH	Rouquancourt – Le Bourget.
18/8/40	Me 110	SD+BH	Le Bourget – Mannnheim Ost.
19/8/40	Me 110	PD+BH	Mannheim Ost – Mannheim Sandhofen.
19/8/40	Me 110	PD+BH	Sandhofen – Mannheim Ost.
20/8/40	Me 110	PD+BH	Mannheim Ost – Le Bourget.
24/8/40	Me 110	L1+NH	Rouquancourt – Rouquancourt. War Flight escorting bomber formation.
25/8/40	Me 110	L1+NL	Rouquancourt – Lessey. War Flight escorting bomber formation. Attacked by Hurricane nr Portland; 38 bullet holes in starboard engine, steering gear and tyre.
26/8/40	Me 110	L1+DL	Rouquancourt – Rouquancourt. War Flight escorting bomber formation. Twice attacked by Spitfires 30 km E Portland; one Spitfire shot down by an Me110.
27/8/40	Me 110	L1+DL	Rouquancourt – Rouquancourt.
28/8/40	Me 110	L1+DL	Rouquancourt – Ligescourt.
29/8/40	Me 110	L1+DL	S London. War Flight, free-lance patrol, saw only a few enemy fighters.
30/8/40	Me 110	L1+DL	War Flight escorting He 111 formation to Aldershot. One Hurricane shot down 12.20 hrs 15 km N Rye. One Hurricane shot down 12.23 hrs 10 km W Rye.
30/8/40	Me 110	L1+DL	Ligescourt – St Omer. War Flight escorting bomber formation to Radlett. Attacked two Hurricanes and one Spitfire. Forced landed at St Omer due to lack of fuel.

1/9/40	Me 110	L1+DL	Ligescourt – St Omer. War Flight escorting bomber formation to SE London. W/T operator shot down a Hurricane.
4/9/40	Me 110	L1+DL	Ligescourt – Ligescourt. War Flight escorting fourteen Me 110 bombers to Vickers Wellington Works, Aldershot. Met about 30 enemy fighters in violent clash over Aldershot before retiring.
6/9/40	Me 110	L1+DL	Ligescourt – Ligescourt. War Flight escorting Me 110 bombers to Vickers Wellington Works at Aldershot. Saw five enemy fighters but no fighting.
7/9/40	Me 110	L1+DL	Ligescourt – Ligescourt. War Flight escorting bomber Geschwader to London. Fifteen enemy fighters and attacked twice but escaped by doing spiral turns; shot at one of the Spitfires.
8/9/40	Me 110	L1+DL	Ligescourt – Ligescourt. War Flight escorting Bomber Geschwader to London. Slight contact with enemy. Three Spitfires. Two Me 109s collided in mid air. AA scored a direct hit on a Do 17. Counted seven parachutes. *(3 Do17s of 5/KG2 see page 366)*

MAP ID 15 (page 368)

| 9 September 1940 | Bf110C-4 | Wn.2137 | 2N+FM | 7/ZG76 |

Munsgore Lane, Borden, near Sittingbourne, Kent. 18.00 hrs.

Aircraft hit by a direct hit by AA fire from 1/58 AA Battery at Twydall. Both of the crew baled out but one was killed by shrapnel and the other left it too late before baling out. Aircraft completely destroyed. No armour or armour plate found.

Pilot: ID: 53585, AW: green, issued by E.103, 30/7/40, FP: L 32337.
Bf: ID: 69010, AW: white, issued by E.17/XII, 23/8/40, FP: L 01402.
Ff: Uffz Georg-Alfred Bierling EKII 69010/13 +. CC 4/54.
Bf: Uffz Friedrich Kurella 53585/178 +. CC 4/55.

The pilot's ID disc was that of Ergänzungs ZG1, along with the Feldpostnummer. The wireless operator's ID disc had been identified with the 4th and 5th Staffeln of ZG1.

The pilot's diary was found with the following entries:
30/8/40   Escorting He111s to Aldershot. Combat.
31/8/40   Escorting Do17s to Cambridge. Combat.
1/9/40   Do 17 Tunbridge Wells.
2/9/40   Do 17 Etaples. Severe fighting.
4/9/40   110 K Gruppe.
8/9/40   Moved to Cherbourg. Called off QBI.   *(Some sources quote this aircraft as Wn.2173)*

Right: Probably a fitting final photo for this volume, another big hole with bits of Bf110 in it. This time 2N+FM at Borden near Sittingbourne.

9 September 1940	Bf110C-2	Wn.3108	2N+EP	9/ZG76	MAP ID 16 (page 368)

At sea - five miles off Newhaven, Sussex. 18.00 hrs.

Started at 17.30 hrs escorting Heinkel He111s. The height during the journey varied between 13,000 and 21,000 ft. When near London, the formation was attacked by Spitfires, the wireless operator being wounded. The pilot tried to get back to France, but was attacked a second time by Hurricanes off Newhaven and eventually came down in the sea.
Markings: E in yellow.
ID: Jgd.Sch.Schleissheim, AW: white, issued by L 32311, 29/8/40, FP: L 01544.
Ff: Fw Hermann Koops.
Bf: Uffz Christian Weiher +. CC 1/86.

The pilot gave his unit as 3/ZG76 but the Feldpostnummer was that of II/ZG 1.
The wireless operator's name was unknown to the pilot, but his body was washed ashore at Lydd, Kent on 2nd October 1940.

The pilot's diary gave the following:
13/8/40   Zerstörerschule, Scheissheim.
23/8/40   In Laval.
26/8/40   Caen – Plymouth.
29/8/40   SW London.
30/8/40   London.
31/8/40   Cambridge.
1/9/40   London.
4/9/40   Escorted bombers to Vickers Works.
8/9/40   Escorted 40 Do17s to London.

9 September 1940	Bf110C-4	Wn.3207	2N+EP	9/ZG76	MAP ID 17 (page 368)

Woodcote Park Avenue, Woodmanstern, Surrey. 18.15 hrs.

The pilot was wounded by a shot near his heart and either baled out or fell out, his parachute failing to open.
ID: 53585, AW: white card with orange back, issued by FP no. L 32311, LGP Frankfurt, 21/7/40, FP: -.
Ff: Ltn Eduard Ostermünchner 53585/19 +. CC 1/327.
Bf: Gefr Werner Zimmermann 53582/32 +. CC 5/64.

The pilot's ID disc had previously been encountered with a number of Messerschmitt Bf110 units including ZG1, 2, 76 and EproGr.210. The Ausweis had not been previously encountered.

Although Messerschmitt Bf110s werke nummers 3108 and 3207, both of 9/ZG76, are recorded as carrying the same fuselage code and both were bought down on the same day, it would be assumed that either one of the aircraft was a spare and there was no time to change the markings, or there was an error in the Quartermaster Generals Returns for the Luftwaffe as it is unlikely that two aircraft from the same unit would carry the same code at the same time.
Alternatively there is some evidence that Wn.3108 could have been 2N+BP, which would then solve the problem which may have been just a simple transcription error.